ISBN: 9781313061131

Published by:
HardPress Publishing
8345 NW 66TH ST #2561
MIAMI FL 33166-2626

Email: info@hardpress.net
Web: http://www.hardpress.net

PASTURE STUDIES:

SOME RESULTS

CONTENTS

INTRODUCTION.

The main object of this publication is to place on record certain results obtained by the writer from the study of pasture herbage. A few of the present results and others have already been embodied in a paper written jointly by Mr. R. G. Stapledon, M.A., and the present writer, and published in the Journal of Agricultural Science (**18**),[1] but the greater part of the results are now published for the first time.

METHODS OF EXAMINATION.

(a) Percentage Frequency.—This method was originally used by Armstrong (**1**), and was adopted by Stapledon (**15**) in a modified form. It has been re-defined as " the number of plants of each species per unit area " expressed in percentages of the total herbage (**18**).

This method has been further modified to some extent by the present writer, as follows :—

(1) The plant unit has been re-defined :

i. For most plants, the plant unit shall consist of any portion of a plant possessing an independent shoot, which can be separated from others with at least three rootlets still attached to it. If a portion possesses six rootlets and it can be separated into two in such a way that each portion possesses three rootlets, then it counts as two plant units.

ii. The plant unit of *Trifolium repens* shall be, " any portion of runner up to three inches in length and bearing functioning rootlets."

iii. The plant unit for *Nardus stricta* shall be as nearly as possible comparable in size to that of *Festuca ovina.*[2]

iv. In a few cases the plant unit used is, " any individual tiller or shoot irrespective of roots." This definition applies to

---

[1] Figures in heavy type and in brackets refer to list of references at the end.
[2] This definition was adopted owing to the plant's peculiar habit. It is obviously unsatisfactory, and in future work it is intended to bring this plant, in spite of its peculiar habit, under the general definition (i.)

Juncus spp., *Carex* spp., *Luzula* spp., *Schoenus nigricans*, and plants of a similar habit.[1]

2. A new turf-sampling mesh was introduced.

In 1916, the 6in. × 6in. mesh previously used for taking specimen turves was partly replaced with a new mesh, 12in. × 1in. This new mesh has since been used exclusively on pastures which are fairly well grazed, and on such it is quite satisfactory.   Where the herbage is rank, the 6in. × 6in. mesh is still used.

(b) Percentage Area.—This method was also originally used by Armstrong (**1**), but the present writer has found it effective and reliable only in the estimation of the area covered by herbs which are easily identified, and, in a pasture, grow quite near the ground.   Only results obtained for *Trifolium repens* by this method will be referred to.

(c) Specific Frequency.—This is a qualitative method introduced by Stapledon (**15**) (**17**).   It has been re-defined as " the number of times a species (without regard to the number of plants of that species), occurs per 100 readings within the 6in. × 6in. mesh (**18**).   This method is exceedingly useful for ascertaining the distribution of plants which are easily identified in pastures, but much less satisfactory in the case of grasses.   The writer has used it mostly on young pastures for ascertaining the distribution of leguminous and other plants which are easily identified *in situ*.

AREAS EXAMINED.

Up till quite recently, relatively little work had been done to ascertain to what extent and for how long, species whose seeds are commonly included in seeds-mixtures used for laying land down to pasture persist in such pastures.

The present writer commenced his investigations along these lines in 1913 on land the history of which was well known to him.

All the areas for which results are here given are situated on the farm of Budloy, near Maenclochog, Pembrokeshire.[2]   This

---

[1] In some respects, these definitions resemble that adopted by Yapp, Johns and Jones (**22**).

[2] A few results obtained elsewhere are given to illustrate certain points.

farm may be described as a mixed hill farm with no natural first, nor even second class land. It is about 160 acres in extent, and varies in altitude from 500ft. to 940ft. Less than half the total area is cultivable.

The soil is of three main types :—

Type i. : Thin, rather light loam, sedentary on shale. Very small areas of this type are found between 500ft. and 600ft., and also between 600ft. and 700ft. while the greater part of the area between 700ft. and 900ft. is of this type.

Type ii. : Thin, slightly heavier loam on local drift. This local drift consists chiefly of shale with some felsite(?) boulders. This soil is of a silty character, and is very liable to cake on the surface when rain follows immediately after thorough cultivation to a fine tilth. Most of the land regularly cultivated and the best permanent pasture fields are on this type.

Type iii. : Thin, acid peat on felsite rock. Most of the land above 800ft. is of this type. All this land is uncultivable, owing to the thin nature of the peat and the presence of felsite blocks.

The character of the herbage on soil-types i. and ii. will be most clearly seen from the tables. The most important arable land weeds on the farm are :—

Agrostis spp.
Chrysanthemum segetum (local).
Galeopsis Tetrahit (local).
Arrhenatherum elatius var. *tuberosum* (local).
Polygonum Persicaria.
Stellaria media.
Cirsium arvense.
Ranunculus repens.

These chiefly occur on soil-type ii. The land on soil-type i. has been little cultivated, but on this *Rumex Acetosella* was a prominent weed in places.

Soil-type iii. carries a distinct type of herbage which may be described as a *Calluna* heath. *Calluna vulgaris* is dominant, but it is accompanied by *Erica Tetralix, Vaccinium Myrtillus, Festuca*

ovina, Deschampsia flexuosa,
Scirpus caespitosus, etc.[1] No quantitative examination of this
heath herbage has been made.

The cultivation of the land on the farm varies somewhat
according to circumstances. As this seems to be important, full
details will be given for each area examined. The main features
are, that the length of the rotation is usually 10 to 15 years, and
that the land is well cultivated and manured while under cultivation, but that it very rarely happens that the entire area which is
seeded down to pasture in any one year has been entirely under
a cleaning crop[2] in the course of that rotation.

The land is always seeded down to grass with a corn cover-
ing crop, usually dredge-corn.[3] Since the rotation is a somewhat
irregular one, no land is laid down to grass in some years.

The seeds-mixtures used on the farm have varied considerably
in recent years, but formerly they were of a simple character.
Fortunately, the species included in all seeds-mixtures used from
1883 to 1917, with the exception of those used in 1901, 1902 and
1903,[4] are known. During this period 23 seeds-mixtures were
used, and the various species and commercial varieties included
are given in Table I.

TABLE I. : Showing the Years in which various " seeds "[5] were
included in Seeds-mixtures on Budloy.

   1. *Lolium perenne* : All seeds-mixtures 1883-1917.

   2. " Broad Red Clover "[6] : All seeds-mixtures except in
1911 and 1912.

   3. *Plantago lanceolata* : 1884, 1887-91, 1898, 1902 (?),
1905, '06, '09, '12.

   4. *Lolium italicum* : 1891, '97, '98, 1906-17.

   5. *Trifolium hybridum* : 1898 (?), 1905-17.

[1] *Calluna vulgaris* is everywhere dominant in the older herbage, but the
abundance of the other species varies in different places according to the slope,
etc. After burning, *Calluna* does not become dominant for a few years.
[2] Potatoes, Mangels, Turnips, etc.
[3] A mixture of barley and oats.
[4] Some details are known for these years also.
[5] The word "seeds" is used throughout in the commercial or common sense.
[6] The Commercial names of the different varieties are given.

6. *Phleum pratense* : 1901, '02, '08, '11, '13-'17.
7. *Dactylis glomerata* : 1903-1917.
8. "Cowgrass" (*Trifolium pratense*) : 1905-'08, 1911-13.
9. *Medicago lupulina* : 1905, '06.
10. *Festuca elatior* : 1908, '13.
11. Ditto   var. *pratensis* : 1908, '13, '17.
12. *F. duriuscula* : 1908-13.
13. *Poa pratensis* : 1908, '16.
14. "White or Dutch Clover" : 1908-13.
15. *Anthyllis Vulneraria* : 1908-17.
16. "Hybrid Cow Clover" : 1909.
17. *Festuca ovina* : 1911.
18. *Cynosurus cristatus* : 1911, '16, '17.
19. *Anthoxanthum odoratum* : 1911.
20. *Medicago sativa* : 1911, '12.
21. *Cichorium Intybus* : 1911, '12, '16, '17.
22. *Poterium Sanguisorba* : 1911, '12.
23. *Carum Petroselinum* : 1911, '12.
24. *Arrhenatherum elatius* : 1912, '13, '17.
25. "Late-flowering Red Clover" : 1912, '16, '17.
26. *Alopecurus pratensis* : 1913.
27. *Poa trivialis* : 1916, '17.
28. "Wild White Clover" : 1916, '17.
29. *Trifolium dubium* : 1916.
30. *Achillea Millefolium* : 1916, '17.

The evolution of the seeds-mixture on this particular farm as shown by these data is seen to have been relatively slow, but even in the absence of expert advice, it had been proceeding prior to 1908. After this, the seeds-mixtures were more or less of an experimental character, although used on the most extensive scale possible on the farm. The details of the seeds-mixtures used on Areas 1-8 are given in Table IV., p.60, except that a few miscellaneous plants are not included.[1]

[1] For these, see under "Individual Species," p. 15 *et seq.*

AREA 1.

Altitude : 650 feet.

Soil : Type ii. (p. 3).

History : In grass 1898-1910 ; oats 1910 ; bastard fallow ; dredge corn 1911 ; oats 1912 ; bastard fallow ; dredge corn 1913, and seeded down to permanent pasture with the seeds-mixture shown in Table IV. The area was well manured with farmyard manure and phosphates during this period of cultivation, but was only partly under a cleaning crop.

Hay was taken in 1914, farmyard manure was applied winter 1914-15, and hay again taken in 1915. It has been continuously grazed since, without further manuring.

AREA 2.   Adjoining Area 1.

Altitude : 700 feet.

Soil : Mostly Type ii. (p. 3), but partly of Type i.

History : In grass 1895-1905 without manuring ; hay 1905 ; oats 1906 ; bastard fallow ; dredge-corn 1907 ; bastard fallow ; partly dredge-corn and partly oats 1908, and then seeded down to grass ; well manured with farmyard manure and phosphates while under cultivation, but no part of it under a cleaning crop ; mown for hay in 1909 and 1910 ; subsequently grazed ; 5 cwt. Basic Slag per acre applied in winter 1913-14. *Cynosurus cristatus* was very prominent in the hay crop of 1905.

The area is bounded to the north by uncultivable land in which *Ulex europaeus* (used for horse fodder) is dominant in most places. In other places, *Rubus* spp., and *Pteris aquilina* are prominent and *Agrostis tenuis, Anthoxanthum odoratum, Dactylis glomerata, Festuca rubra, Holcus lanatus,* and *Cynosurus cristatus* are more or less abundant.

AREA 3.   Part of the same field as Area 2.

Altitude : 650 feet.

Soil : Type ii. (p. 3).

History : As for Area 2 up till 1905 ; oats 1905, and under cultivation for five successive seasons, during which time the whole area was under a cleaning crop ; well manured while under cultivation ; seeded down to pasture 1909 ; mown for hay 1910, and subsequently grazed without further manuring.

AREA 4.   Adjoining Areas 1 and 2.

Altitude : 675 feet.
Soil : Type ii. (p. 3).
History : In grass probably for about 10 years prior to 1898 ; ploughed in the spring of 1898 and put through a course of cultivation similar to that of Area 1 ; laid down to grass in 1903 ; mown for hay in 1904 ; subsequently grazed without further manuring.

The details of the seeds-mixture used are not known, but it is known that *Lolium perenne, Dactylis glomerata*, " Broad Red Clover," and probably *Plantago lanceolata* were included.

AREA 5.   Adjoining Area 1 diagonally.

Altitude : 600 feet.
Soil : Type ii. (p. 3) ; slightly deeper and lighter than Area 1.
History : Grazed continuously with very little manuring for at least 50 years prior to 1903 ; oats 1903 ; bastard fallow ; dredge-corn 1904 ; oats 1905 ; bastard fallow ; dredge-corn 1906, when it was seeded down ; well manured while under cultivation, and partly under a cleaning crop in 1904 and 1905 ; mown for hay 1907 ; dressed with lime compost winter 1907-8 ; mown for hay 1908 ; subsequently grazed without manure.

Holcus lanatus was very prominent in the 1908 hay crop.

AREA 6.
Altitude : 850 feet.
Soil : Type i. (p. 3).
History : It is known to have been under cultivation about 1855, and that during that period of cultivation it was partly under a cleaning crop.   It was also manured at that time with peat

ashes and guano,[1] and to some extent with farmyard manure, but there is no evidence to show that it was limed.

The conditions under which the area was then laid down to grass are not known, nor its treatment in the years immediately following.   It is known, however, that in a few years it was again merged in the sheep walk of which it previously formed a part, and was allowed to revert to its natural herbage without any inter-ference.   About 1898, however, it was given a light dressing of Basic Slag, which had very little apparent effect.   By this time the herbage was of a grass-heath type, dotted with *Ulex europaeus* and a few *Ulex Gallii* bushes closely trimmed by sheep.   Patches of *Calluna vulgaris* also occurred on the thinnest soil.   After 1898 *Lotus corniculatus* colonies were fairly common, and some weak *Trifolium repens* plants were to be found.

The area was ploughed in the winter of 1906-7 ; oats 1907 ; oats 1908 ; bastard fallow ; partly dredge-corn and partly rape 1909 ; oats 1910 ; bastard fallow ; dredge-corn 1911, and seeded down to pasture; well manured with farmyard manure and phosphates, and to a slight extent with kainit and nitrate of soda while under cultivation ; mown for hay 1912 ; subsequently grazed, chiefly by cattle up till 1918, when it was again thrown open to sheep and very heavily grazed.   In 1918 it was also badly scorched in the drought of the early summer, as the soil is thin, on a strong slope with a southern aspect.   A dressing of Basic Slag was applied in the spring of 1916.

AREA 7.   Part of the same field as Area 6.

Altitude : 750 feet.
Soil : Type i. (p. 3).
History : As for Area 6 up till 1906 ; ploughed, winter 1907-8 and put through exactly the same course of cultivation as Area 6, with similar manuring ; laid down to grass 1912, but, as will be seen from Table IV., the seeds-mixture used differed widely from

[1] This fact is of considerable interest, as the first cargo of this manure only reached England in 1840 (5), and the farm is in a very inaccessible locality.

that used on Area 6. The after treatment was also different in that Area 7 was not mown for hay.

AREA 8. Adjoining Area 6.

Altitude : 850 feet.

Soil : Type i. (p. 3).

History : This area has formed part of the sheep walk already referred to for an unknown period (probably over a hundred years), but there is evidence that it was under cultivation at some remote period. The presence of imperfectly burnt limestone cores shows that it has been limed, but otherwise it is not known to have been manured. At the time of examination, a considerable proportion of the field was over-run by *Ulex europaeus*,[1] but on the part examined only scattered bushes were found, and in between, the herbage was typical grass heath.

It will be seen that these eight areas fall into two clearly defined groups. Areas 1-5 are mainly on soil-type ii., and have generally been regularly cultivated on the long rotation system. The slope of these is also much more gentle than that of Areas 6-8, and they are much more easily accessible.

Areas 6-8 are on soil-type i. The character of the herbage natural to these situations at a late stage of stabilisation when untended is shown by the analyses of the herbage of Area 8 (Tables IV. and V., pp. 16a, 16b).

The results obtained for these eight areas are especially valuable on account of the facts that some of them have been repeatedly examined, and that the soil conditions for each group are almost perfectly comparable. The examinations in each year were also made for all areas in August and September.

Further particulars are given in Table II. (p. 10).

---

[1] It seems probable that the plant had been sown on part of the field for fodder purposes.

TABLE II.

Showing Altitude, Soil-type, and Extent of each Area, the Age of the Pasture, and Method of Examination employed.*

Area	1	2	3	4	5	6	7	8
Altitude	650ft.	700ft.	650ft.	675ft.	600ft.	850ft.	750ft.	850ft.
Soil-type	ii.	ii.	ii.	ii.	ii.	i.	i.	i.
Extent	5 ac.	5 ac.	3 ac.	3 ac.	6 ac.	6 ac.	3 ac.	2 ac.
Age								
3½	Sp. fr.	—	—	—	—	—	—	—
4½	Both	—	—	—	—	P. c. fr.	Sp. fr.	—
5½	P.c. fr.	Both	—	—	—	Both	P.c. fr.	—
6½	—	P.c. fr.	—	—	—	P.c. fr.	,,	—
7½	—	,,	Sp. fr.	—	—	,,	—	—
8½	—	Both	P.c. fr.	—	—	—	—	—
9½	—	P.c. fr.	P.c. fr,	—	—	—	—	—
10½	—	Both	—	—	Sp. fr.	—	—	—
13½	—	—	—	Both	—	—	—	—
100 (?)	—	—	—	—	—	—	—	Both

*The altitudes are given in feet and the age in years. Sp. fr. = Specific Frequency method ; P.c. fr. = Percentage Frequency method. For convenience, these abbreviations are largely used in the text.

SEEDS-MIXTURES.

The chief constituents of the seeds-mixtures used for all these areas except Areas 4 and 8 are shown in Table IV. (p. 16a). The full details of that used on Area 4 are not known. It was, however, fairly simple, and included no grasses except *Lolium* spp. and *Dactylis glomerata*. It also included *Trifolium pratense* ("Broad Red Clover"), and possibly, but not probably, *T*, *hybridum,* but no other clover seed.   It also probably included the seed of *Plantago lanceolata.*

Nothing is known as to the character of the seeds-mixture used on Area 8.

AGGREGATE RESULTS.

TABLE III.

Aggregate Results obtained by the Percentage Frequency Method.

Area.	Altitude (feet).	Age (years).	Gramineae.		Leguminosae.		Other Orders.	
			Sown.	Not Sown.	Sown.	Not Sown.	Sown.	Not Sown.
1	650	$4\frac{1}{2}$	19·7	36·7	27·5	0·2	—	15·9
1	,,	$5\frac{1}{2}$	13·2	36·2	31·8	0·1	—	18·8
2	700	$5\frac{1}{2}$	10·5	56·4	12·4	0·4	—	20·5
2	,,	$6\frac{1}{2}$	8·0	58·3	17·4	0·7	—	15·5
2	,,	$7\frac{1}{2}$	7·5	52·0	18·7	0·9	—	20·9
2	,,	$8\frac{1}{2}$	6·4	55·0	18·2	0·7	—	19·4
2	,,	$9\frac{1}{2}$	4·8	64·4	15·7	0·8	—	14·1
2	,,	$10\frac{1}{2}$	4·1	63·3	15·9	0·3	—	16·5
3	650	$8\frac{1}{2}$	8·5	49·4	18·0	0·3	0·7	23·1
3	,,	$9\frac{1}{2}$	5·0	48·4	23·1	1·3	—	22·2
4*	675	$13\frac{1}{2}$	1·8	64·0	0·4	15·9	2·2	16·2
6	850	$4\frac{1}{2}$	73·3	8·8	8·7	3·2	0·1	6·0
6	,,	$5\frac{1}{2}$	51·5	12·2	27·6	0·9	—	7·7
6	,,	$6\frac{1}{2}$	47·8	15·0	24·7	3·0	—	9·3
6	,,	$7\frac{1}{2}$	48·9	32·4	8·9	1·1	—	8·7
7	750	$5\frac{1}{2}$	11·1	64·2	10·9	3·8	0·9	9·3
7	,,	$6\frac{1}{2}$	5·7	74·7	9·9	0·4	0·2	8·8
8	850	100·(?)	78·5		3·4		18·1	

*Details of seeds-mixture used not known.

It is obviously impossible directly to compare the results for Areas 1-5 with those for Areas 6-8 as the natural factors are different for the two groups. For each of the groups, however, the soil and altitude factors may be regarded as relatively constant, and for Areas 6 and 7 the treatment of the land was so nearly similar that this also may be considered almost constant. The treatment of Areas 1-5, although mainly similar, was different in respects which may be of considerable importance, while the composition of the seeds-mixture varied considerably for each area.

The aggregate results obtained by the P.c. fr. method are given in terms of sown species and those not sown, but where the seeds-mixture is widely different, the significance of these aggregate results becomes less. This is due to the fact that in no case probably would the soil be quite free from living plants or at least of seeds which might produce plants in the young pasture, when laid down to grass (3). In addition, no provision could be made against the recolonisation of the ground by indigenous plants whose seeds might be introduced by natural means.

The term "sown species" used here must therefore include all the plants of those species the seeds of which had been included in the seeds-mixture, whether their presence be the result of sowing the seed or not.

The difficulty which occurs under this consideration is however very much reduced by the fact that most of the areas have been examined in successive years.

GRAMINEAE.

(a) Sown.

As will be seen from Table III., the tendency on all these areas is towards a decrease in the proportion of sown grasses from year to year. This is very clearly shown by the results for Area 2 where there was a steady decrease from 10·5 per cent. at $5\frac{1}{2}$ years to 4·1 per cent. at $10\frac{1}{2}$ years. Assuming that this decrease continued at the average rate of the last three years for the further period of three years (up till $13\frac{1}{2}$ years), the sown grasses would then have been reduced to less than 1 per cent. This would apparently not occur, as on Area 4 there was still a P.c. fr. of 1·8 at 13½ years.

The large decrease on Area 1 from 19·7 per cent. at 4½ years to 13·2 per cent. at 5½ years, strongly suggests that the decrease on these areas was at first rapid, but became slower later on. The results for Areas 1 and 3 do not agree with those for Area 2 at corresponding periods however, although there was relatively little difference between Areas 2 and 3 at 9½ years. These differences may be due either to the different treatment given to the areas, or to the composition of the seeds-mixtures used.

The results for Area 6 are in marked contrast with those for the other areas, even with those for Area 7, which was in most respects comparable with it. A P.c. fr. of 73·3 at 4½ years is exceptionally high, as also are the other results in succeeding years on the same area.[1]

Areas 6 and 7 had similar soil conditions, and their treatment was mainly similar throughout. The only difference in treatment was, that Area 6 was mown for hay at 1¼ years while Area 7 was grazed. It may be that this placed Area 7 at a disadvantage— that by being grazed in the first season a large proportion of the sown grasses was uprooted. This is probably not the case, as in this, and even in the following year, it was grazed with cattle only.

The difference in altitude would be expected to give the advantage to Area 7,[2] so that apparently the chief cause of the difference was the difference in the composition of the seeds-mixtures.

(b) Not sown.

Areas 2 and 4 appear to agree fairly closely, but again there was a considerable difference between Areas 2 and 3 and between Areas 1 and 2. These differences are probably partially explained when the individual species are considered,[3] but they may also have some significance in connection with the treatment of the

[1] Cf. (18).
[2] This would perhaps depend however on the nature of the seeds sown.
[3] See *Anthoxanthum odoratum*, p. 27, especially.

land.   No part of Area 2, in which the unsown grasses were most prominent, was under a cleaning crop while under cultivation; Area 1 was partly under a cleaning crop, while Area 3 was entirely under such a crop.   Areas 1 and 3 were not examined at corresponding ages, and it is possible that the unsown grasses had increased rapidly on Area 3.   It may be borne in mind, however, that Area 1 was dressed with farmyard manure *after* it was laid down to grass.

In spite of the fact that Area 6 had not been under a cleaning crop, the percentage of unsown grasses was exceedingly low up to $6\frac{1}{2}$ years.   In the following year they increased rapidly, but this was probably due to (*a*) change in the method of grazing, (*b*) a period of drought (see p. 8).   At $7\frac{1}{2}$ years, however, these grasses were very much less developed on Area 6 than on Area 7 even at $5\frac{1}{2}$ years.   The increase on the latter area at $6\frac{1}{2}$ years was probably due to the same cause as the increase on Area 6 at $7\frac{1}{2}$ years.

LEGUMINOSAE.

The results for Areas 1 and 2 in respect of sown leguminous plants differ very markedly.   Other peculiar features of the results are, the sudden changes both on Areas 2 and 6, and the difference between Area 4 and all the others, but as this is a question mainly of *Trifolium repens*, these features are better pursued when the individual species are discussed.

OTHER ORDERS.

The seeds of some plants belonging to other Natural Orders were included in the seeds-mixtures for some of the areas.[1]   The P.c. fr. results obtained for these plants are almost negligible, so they will be considered under the various species.

The aggregate results for the unsown species do not show any regular sequence.   The most marked feature is the difference between the area groups, 1-4 and 6-8.   The results for Area 8 show that in the old grass-heath the miscellaneous plants formed as high a proportion of the herbage as on Areas 1-4, but on Areas

[1] See under " Individual Species," p. 15 *et seq.*

6 and 7 they formed a much smaller proportion. As will be seen from the detailed results (Table IV.), although Area 8 agreed with Areas 1-4 in the proportion of these plants, it differed markedly from them in other respects. It would appear therefore that the cause of the low figures for Areas 6 and 7 is, that the heath-plants proper had been very largely eradicated, and that for some reason they had not been fully replaced by others.

The relatively high results for Area 3 may be connected with the fact that the area was under a cleaning crop while under cultivation, and that therefore these plants had not to compete to the same extent with other indigenous plants. On the whole, these plants seem to show some tendency to decrease on Area 2, but on Area 4 at 13½ years their total P.c. fr. was higher than on Area 2 at 9½ years and at 10½ years.

INDIVIDUAL SPECIES.

GRAMINEAE.

Results for Gramineae were obtained by the Percentage Frequency method only. These results and also the weight of seed sown per acre are given in Table IV., p. 16a.

Lolium italicum.

This grass is usually regarded as either an annual or a biennial, so that, although the seed was included in the seeds-mixtures for most of the present areas, since none of them was examined within the first three years it is not surprising that the grass should not have been recorded.

Lolium perenne.

Results obtained by Armstrong in the Market Harborough district of Leicestershire and Northamptonshire (1) show that this grass may contribute largely to the herbage of some pastures. On different types of pastures, his results were as follows :—

On an extreme type of poor pasture, 1 per cent.
On other inferior old pastures, 14·1 to 44·6 per cent.
On excellent recent pastures, 28 to 47·2 per cent.
On first rate old pastures, 33·4 to 39·3 per cent.

The highest percentage frequency result obtained by the present writer was 20·2 on a good old pasture at an altitude of 50 feet,[1] and the P.c. fr. of the grass on the best pasture examined by him was 4·6.[2]

The present areas are not comparable with any of these. Armstrong's results were obtained by a different method, while the conditions of soil and altitude were much more favourable on the other two areas mentioned than on those for which the results are here given.

The grass was sown on all the present areas, with the possible exception of Area 8, in quantities ranging from 6 to 18 lb. per acre.[3] Since the grass has been sown on that part of the farm which is under regular rotation for many years (Table I.) it is not known whether it is truly indigenous to Areas 1-5 or not, but, as shown by the results for Area 8, it is not indigenous to Areas 6, 7 and 8.

The highest P.c. fr. for Areas 1-4 was 10·3 on Area 1 at $4\frac{1}{2}$ years.   On this area it decreased to 6·1 per cent. at $5\frac{1}{2}$ years, and at that time it was slightly less abundant than on Area 2 at the corresponding period, although a heavier seeding had been given to the former area.

On Area 2 its decrease was slower from $5\frac{1}{2}$ years onwards than on Area 1 at an earlier date, but it was continuous and regular, so that at $10\frac{1}{2}$ years it had a P.c. fr. of only 3·0.   It was rather more abundant on Area 3 at $8\frac{1}{2}$ years than on Area 2 at the corresponding period, but the results for the two areas at $9\frac{1}{2}$ years are almost identical in spite of the difference in quantity of seed sown, while on Area 4 at $13\frac{1}{2}$ years there was still a P.c. fr. of 1·1.

These results indicate quite clearly that under the conditions of these areas the grass decreases from year to year, at least up to about $13\frac{1}{2}$ years, but that even in that length of time it does not completely disappear, and that, in fact, up to about $8\frac{1}{2}$ years it may be quite as abundant as in some excellent Welsh pastures (see above).

[1] College Farm, Aber, Bangor.
[2] 18 years old pasture in Anglesey at 200 feet.
[3] Probably more on Area 4.

TABLE IV.—Gramineae and Leguminosae.   Seeds s(

AREA.	1			2						
	Seeds-Mixture	4½ yrs.	5½ yrs.	Seeds-Mixture	5½ yrs.	6½ yrs.	7½ yrs.	8½ yrs.	9½ yrs.	10½ yis.
olium italicum	5	—	—	5	—	—	—	—	—	—
. perenne	15	10·3	6·1	12	6·6	6·2	5·4	4·7	3·6	3·0
Dactylis glomerata ...	5	5·5	4·3	3	2·1	1·4	0·7	0·9	0·5	0·5
estuca elatior et var. ...	3	1·3	2·1	⅓	0·3	0·2	0·5	0·1	0·4	—
. duriuscula	3	—	—	2½	—	—	—	—	—	—
. ovina	—	—	—	—	—	—	0·1	—	—	—
. rubra	—	2·9	4·4	—	7·9	6·1	7·7	5·9	7·1	7·9
hleum pratense ...	4	1·2	0·5	3	1·5	0·2	0·3	0·5	0·3	0·2
rrhenatherum elatius ..	2	0·3	0·2	—	—	—	—	—	—	—
lopecurus pratensis ...	1	1·1	—	—	—	—	—	—	—	—
oa pratensis	—	—	—	¼	—	—	0·6	0·2	—	0·4
. trivialis	—	3·8	2·3	—	1·3	2·0	2·0	4·0	2·3	4·7
. annua	—	8·4	0·6	—	—	—	T	—	—	—
Cynosurus cristatus ...	—	T	3·8	—	8·1	9·2	10·9	9·4	12·2	14·7
nthoxanthum odoratum ...	—	2·5	2·3	—	18·9	21·2	11·3	12·1	12·2	7·0
grostis spp.	—	14·3	13·5	—	17·5	17·1	14·9	15·2	21·9	21·5
Iolcus lanatus	—	4·8	9·3	—	2·5	2·6	5·0	8·2	8·7	6·8
rrhenatherum elatius var. ...	—	—	T	—	0·1	0·1	0·1	0·2	—	0·7
ira caryophyllea ...	—	—	—	—	0·1	—	—	—	—	—
ieglingia decumbens ...	—	—	—	—	—	—	—	—	—	—
" Broad Red Clover " ...	½	} —		2	} —	T	T	—	—	—
" Cowgrass " ...	1½			2						
" Hybrid Cow Clover " ...	—	—	—	—	—	—	—	—	—	—
" Late-flowering Red Clover"	—	·-	—	—	—	—	—	—	—	—
rifolium hybridum ...	1	—	—	1½	—	—	—	—	—	—
" White or Dutch Clover " ...	½	27·5	31·8	2	12·4	17·4	18·7	18·2	15·7	15·9
nthyllis Vulneraria ...	1	—	—	¼	—	—	—	—	—	—
Iedicago sativa... ...	—	—	—	—	—	—	—	—	—	—
I. lupulina	—	—	—	—	—	—	—	—	—	—

*T='

TABLE V.—Percentage Frequency and Specific Frequency

AREAS.	1		2						3		4	Percentage Frequencies.
Age of Pasture (years).	4½	5½	5½	6½	7½	8½	9½	10½	8½	9½	13½	
Trifolium pratense[1]	—	—	—	T[2]	T	—	—	—	T	—	0·4	
T. hybridum[1]	—	—	—	—	—	—	—	—	—	—	—	
T. repens[1]	27·5	31·8	12·4	17·4	18·7	18·2	15·7	15·9	18·0	23·1	15·1	
Lotus spp.	—	T	0·3	0·4	0·3	0·7	0·8	0·3	0·3	0·7	0·8	
Plantago lanceolata	—	T	0·4	0·2	—	0·2	0·4	0·8	0·7[3]	T	2·2	
Achillea Millefolium	—	—	0·9	0·9	1·4	2·2	2·3	1·9	1·3	0·7	1·4	
Ranunculus repens	3·6	3·6	3·6	1·3	1·1	1·0	1·1	2·0	2·7	3·0	0·2	
Bellis perennis	5·5	5·4	7·3	4·4	5·2	6·1	2·0	3·7	6·0	7·8	2·3	
Prunella vulgaris	3·3	2·7	2·8	2·6	5·9	4·6	3·6	4·3	9·2	5·9	5·6	
Cerastium vulgatum	1·5	1·7	1·2	0·6	0·2	0·2	0·7	0·2	0·4	0·3	0·2	
Sagina procumbens	1·3	3·9	2·5	4·1	6·2	2·8	1·8	1·0	1·8	2·4	0·3	
Luzula campestris	—	0·3	0·3	0·8	0·1	0·7	1·1	0·6	—	0·5	2·5	
Potentilla erecta	—	—	0·2	0·1	0·2	0·3	0·2	0·2	—	0·2	0·1	
Leontodon autumnalis	0·3	0·5	—	0·3	0·2	0·6	0·5	0·9	0·6	0·2	2·0	
Senecio Jacobaea	0·4	0·6	—	—	—	0·1	—	0·2	0·4	0·6	0·1	
Rumex Acetosa	T[2]	—	0·1	—	T	—	—	T	—	T	0·2	
Centaurea nigra	T	—	—	T	—	0·1	0·4	—	T	—	0·5	
Plantago major	T	T	0·1	—	—	—	—	—	T	—	—	
Rumex Acetosella	—	0·1	—	—	—	T	—	—	—	—	—	
Potentilla anserina	—	—	0·2	0·1	0·1	0·1	—	T	0·3	T	0·1	
Taraxacum vulgare	—	T	0·2	—	0·2	0·3	T	0·5	—	0·2	0·1	
Chrysanthemum Leucanthemum	—	—	0·5	0·1	T	—	—	—	—	—	—	
Polygala vulgaris	—	—	—	—	0·1	0·1	—	—	—	—	—	
Veronica officinalis	—	—	—	—	—	T	—	—	—	—	—	
Viola canina	—	—	—	—	—	—	—	—	—	—	—	
Hieracium Pilosella	—	—	—	—	—	—	—	—	—	0·4	—	
Euphrasia officinalis	—	—	—	T	—	—	—	—	—	—	—	
Thymus Serpyllum	—	—	—	—	—	—	—	—	—	—	—	
Galium hercynicum	—	—	—	—	—	—	—	—	—	—	—	
Calluna vulgaris	—	—	—	—	—	—	—	—	—	—	—	

[1] See Table IV. for quantities of seed sown.   [2] T = Traces.   [3]]

They also suggest that the decrease is rapid up to the fifth year, and that after, there is no definite relationship between the amount of seed sown, and the P.c. fr. of the grass, at least where not less than 8 lb. per acre is sown.

Since the grass is exotic to Areas 6 to 8, it is interesting to note that after a lighter seeding it had a higher P.c. fr. on Area 6 than on Area 1 at $4\frac{1}{2}$ years. Here, however, there was a greater decrease in the following year, and a further decrease in the next year. At $7\frac{1}{2}$ years its P.c. fr. on Area 6 had fallen to 1·8, but the system of grazing had then been changed, and the sudden decrease from $6\frac{1}{2}$ years to $7\frac{1}{2}$ years is probably connected with this, and possibly also with the fact that the area suffered rather severely from drought during this period.[1]

With a light seeding (6 lb. per acre) the grass was but slightly represented on Area 7 at $5\frac{1}{2}$ years, and it was not recorded on this area at $6\frac{1}{2}$ years.

The difference in the amount of seed sown on Areas 6 and 7 was considerable, but it does not seem alone sufficient to account for the difference in the P.c. fr. of the grass on the two areas at corresponding periods.

From the results for Area 6 it is seen, however, that even where not indigenous the grass may persist in fair quantity up to $6\frac{1}{2}$ years, and in some quantity up to at least $7\frac{1}{2}$ years in spite of very heavy grazing with sheep at the end of this period.

Since the presence of the grass in the pasture was desired, these results, (with the possible exception of those for Area 7), fully justify the inclusion of the seed in the seeds-mixture, but at the same time they show that under these conditions the grass does not form a very high proportion of the total herbage after a few years, as on Area 1 it was the second most plentiful grass at $4\frac{1}{2}$ years, while on Area 2 at $10\frac{1}{2}$ years it had fallen to the seventh place, and on Area 6 it had fallen from second place at $4\frac{1}{2}$ years to sixth place at $7\frac{1}{2}$ years.

[1] Stapledon, however, found the grass " wonderfully resistant and persistent " in drought (15).

Dactylis glomerata.

The highest percentage obtained by Armstrong for this grass was 9·5 on one of the inferior old pastures examined by him (**I**). On another inferior old pasture he found only 0·9 per cent., while on first-rate old pasture it ranged from 0·2 per cent. to 4·5 per cent.

On the best pasture examined by the present writer its P.c. fr. was 1·1,[1] while it was not recorded on some of the best old pastures examined. The highest P.c. fr. obtained was 9·5 on a four-year-old pasture after a seeding of 8 lb. per acre.[2]

The seed of the grass was not included in the seeds-mixtures used on the farm on which the present areas are situated until 1903, but the grass was more or less abundant in a permanent hay meadow and along hedgerows up to 700 to 750 feet even before this, so that it may be regarded as more or less strongly indigenous to situations up to 700 feet.

The seed was included in the seeds-mixtures for all the present areas except Area 8.

On Areas 1-4 the highest P.c. fr. obtained was 5·5 on Area 1 at 4½ years. It decreased somewhat on this area in the following year, but even then it was considerably higher than on Area 2 (where a lighter seeding had been given) at the corresponding date. On Area 2 it decreased fairly rapidly up to 7½ years, but it still had a P.c. fr. of 0·5 at 10½ years.

On Area 4, it had persisted rather better apparently, but it is not known what quantity of seed had been sown on this area. It had also persisted better on Area 3 than on Area 2. This may be due to the fact that Area 3 had been more thoroughly cleaned while under cultivation.

Although not indigenous to Areas 6 and 7, the grass was established on these areas even better than on Areas 1-4. On Area 7 especially it had a very high P.c. fr. at 5½ years, while on Area 6 it appeared to be holding its ground from 4½ years to 6½ years. As in the case of *Lolium perenne*, however, it decreased

[1] Anglesey, 200 feet, 18 years.
[2] College Farm, Aberystwyth, 400 feet.

considerably both on Area 6 and on Area 7 under the influence of heavy sheep grazing and (or) drought in 1918.

The results for all these areas taken together suggest that the grass has held its own better on the lighter and drier soil (Areas 6 and 7), and there is some indication also that there may be a distinct relationship between the amount of seed sown and the P.c. fr. of the grass for some years where the other conditions are fairly equal. There is a suggestion, however, that in some cases at least, thorough cleaning of the land is advantageous to the grass (Area 3), although on Area 7 it was by far the most successful sown grass.

Festuca elatior et var. *pratensis.*

These grasses were only recorded on one of the grazed pastures examined by Armstrong, and on this they formed 1 per cent. of the herbage (1).

On the best pasture examined by the writer, they had a P.c. fr. of 6, but they have not been recorded on any of the other old pastures examined. Their presence to the extent of 6 per cent. on the pasture referred to may not mean that they were indigenous. The pasture was but 18 years old, and they may have persisted from sowing. It is more probable, however, that their presence was due to the fact that cattle are regularly winter-fed on the field, and the seed might be repeatedly introduced in the hay. That this is at least possible is shown by the fact that although the grasses are completely exotic to Areas 1-8 and even to the district, they appeared in small quantity on a permanent hay meadow on the farm in a few years after the seed had first been sown on Area 2.

Only a very small quantity of seed was sown as an experiment on Area 2, but the grasses were recorded at each examination up to $9\frac{1}{2}$ years.

On Area 3 a heavier seeding was given, and although the P.c. fr. was low at $4\frac{1}{2}$ years, it was slightly higher than that given by a heavier seeding of *Phleum pratense* (Table IV., p. 16*a*), and in the following year the difference was still greater as the *Festuca* spp. had increased while *Phleum pratense* had decreased.

Thus it is shown that although exotic, one or the other or both these grasses may persist to some extent up to $9\frac{1}{2}$ years under the conditions prevailing on these areas.

Festuca duriuscula.[1]

Festuca duriuscula is the commercial name under which the seed of a variety of *F. ovina* ~~stock~~ was sold before the war.[2] It is said by Hunter (**7**) to be the seed of *F. ovina* (L.), var. *duriuscula* (Koch), but in any case it is different in many respects from any fine-leaved fescue found by the present writer to be indigenous to any of the present areas, and even to any areas in any part of Wales investigated by him.

As will be seen from Table IV., its seed was included in the seeds-mixtures for several of the present areas, but even though sown in quantities from 2 to 3 lb. per acre on Areas 1-3 the grass was not recorded on any of these areas.

On Areas 6 and 7 it was somewhat more successful. On Area 6 it was not separated from other varieties of *F. ovina* which may have been present at $4\frac{1}{2}$ years, but after a seeding of 2 lb. each of this variety and another commercial variety of *F. ovina*, the total P.c. fr. was only 2·7. It is probable, however, that this was mainly *F. duriuscula*, as in other years other varieties were only present in very small quantities, and *F. duriuscula* was decreasing at such a rate that at $7\frac{1}{2}$ years it was represented by only 0·3 per cent.

On Area 7 the grass had a P.c. fr. of 2·7 at $5\frac{1}{2}$ years, but here also it decreased to 1·2 per cent. by the following year.

These results show that the grass is useless for such situations as Areas 1-4, at least after $4\frac{1}{2}$ years, and that even on situations such as 6 and 7, it is of relatively little value. They certainly do not justify the claims generally made for the grass (**2**), (**7**), (**19**).

---

[1] The results for the various forms of fine-leaved fescues are not given separately by Armstrong (**1**).

[2] Much of the seed sold in recent years under this name is that of quite a different grass—probably even a different species. These grasses have been the subject of a special investigation by the writer for some time.

Festuca ovina.

Seeds sown under this name apparently may be those of any species or variety of fine-leaved fescue which are available in quantity. Those sold as *F. ovina tenuifolia* usually conform to a distinct type.

It is not known which of these types was sown on Area 6, but in view of the fact that at $5\frac{1}{2}$ years only 0·1 per cent. of *F. ovina* was recorded, this is of little importance. In the two years which followed, the grass completely disappeared, although, as shown by the fact that it had a P.c. fr. of 16·3 on the old grass-heath of Area 8 adjoining, the grass is strongly indigenous.

This shows, not only that the sown variety was valueless for this situation, but that even the indigenous variety had not re-colonised the ground to an appreciable extent at $7\frac{1}{2}$ years.

On Area 7, where no seed of this name was sown, traces were found at $5\frac{1}{2}$ years, and a percentage frequency of 1·3 at $6\frac{1}{2}$ years, so that evidently for some reason the grass was re-colonising this area at a faster rate than Area 6. This may be chiefly due to the difference in the competing plants, especially the great development of *Cynosurus cristatus* on Area 6.

Festuca rubra.

A creeping variety of this grass is indigenous to Areas 1-4, and it may also be found in very small quantities in the shade of gorse bushes on Area 8. It is probable therefore that it was also to be found to a slight extent on Areas 6 and 7 in similar situations in the original grass-heath. The results for Area 8, however, show that it is not indigenous to the open grass-heath.

The seed of this creeping variety is not obtainable commercially, and the seed of no variety of *F. rubra* was sown on any of these areas. Yet, on Area 2 especially, it formed an important part of the herbage (7·9 per cent.) even at $5\frac{1}{2}$ years, and with some fluctuation in the intervening years, it had exactly the same P.c. fr. at $10\frac{1}{2}$ years.

On Area 1, on the other hand, it had only a P.c. fr. of 4·4 at $5\frac{1}{2}$ years, while the highest for Area 3 was only 2·8 at $8\frac{1}{2}$ years.

Observation has shown that where this creeping **variety** is strongly indigenous it may prove a rather troublesome arable land weed, and therefore, unless the land is rigorously cleaned while under cultivation, the grass may persist bodily. Even where the land is put under a cleaning crop, small portions of the rhizomes may survive. It would be expected therefore that under conditions otherwise equal the grass would be most prevalent in a young pasture where the land had been least perfectly cleaned.

The results for Areas 1-3 perfectly agree with this. Area 2 was not even partly under a cleaning crop ; Area 1 was partly under a cleaning crop while Area 3 was entirely under such a crop.

A percentage frequency of 8·6 at 13½ years on Area 4, which had been partly under a cleaning crop, does not contradict the explanation, as here the grass had had a longer period to recolonise the ground.

The fact that Areas 2 and 4 agree so closely, suggests that on this land, under the conditions prevailing, the grass reaches a certain stability at about 7 to 9 per cent. of the total herbage.

On Areas 6 and 7 the grass, as might have been expected from the fact that it is only weakly indigenous, was but poorly represented. On Area 6 it had a P.c. fr. of 1·0 at 4½ years, but traces only were left at 6½ years, and it was not recorded at 7½ years. This suggests that it was gradually decreasing from a more prominent position occupied prior to 4½ years. Since the area was not under a cleaning crop, the shade provided by the growing corn and by the hay crop would probably favour its development, but when open pasture conditions followed, it rapidly decreased.

The results for Area 7 do not confirm this theory, as here traces only were found at 5½ years, and a P.c. fr. of 1·3 at 6½ years. This area was, however, much less well grazed than Area 6, and it is possible that the shade provided by the rough *Agrostis* herbage was sufficient for its development.

In no case was there any indication that the grass is rejected by stock, so that the only apparent objection to it is its presence as an arable land weed.

Phleum pratense.

This grass is a complete exotic to all the present areas, and its seed was only introduced to the farm in 1901.[1] Its seed was sown on Areas 1, 2, 3 and 6 in quantities from 2 lb. to 4 lb. per acre.

It was prominent in the hay crop taken from Area 2 at $2\frac{1}{4}$ years, but at $5\frac{1}{2}$ years it had only a P.c. fr. of 1·5, and in the next year it decreased to 0·2. Even at $10\frac{1}{2}$ years, however, it had not completely disappeared.

With a somewhat heavier seeding its initial history was somewhat similar on Area 1, but here and on Area 3 its decrease was rather more rapid.

On Area 6, in spite of the drier situation, it had higher percentage frequencies than on Area 1 at corresponding periods, although the seeding was lighter. It was not recorded on this area at $7\frac{1}{2}$ years.

Apparently therefore, this was one of the least satisfactory grasses sown, but it evidently does persist for some years even on these situations. Here it seems to be more valuable for hay than in a pasture.

Arrhenatherum elatius.

The typical species is an exotic to these areas, but its seed was included in the seeds-mixtures for Areas 1 and 7. It was not recorded on Area 7, and its highest P.c. fr. on Area 1 was 0·3 after a seeding of 2 lb. per acre. This grass is therefore apparently of very little value for these situations.

Its variety, *A. elatius tuberosum*, is indigenous to Areas 1-4, and on these areas is a more or less troublesome arable land weed. In these pastures, its highest P.c. fr. was 0·7 on Area 2 at $10\frac{1}{2}$ years, and its next highest was 0·3 on Area 4 at $13\frac{1}{2}$ years Pasturing conditions, therefore, do not exterminate it, but even if it were a desirable pasture plant, it was not sufficiently abundant

[1] The grass must be regarded as a complete exotic in spite of the fact that for several years a small colony, about a foot in diameter, existed in a very old pasture field on the farm, which was at that time continuously mown for hay. This field was remote from the present areas.

on these areas to counterbalance its objectionable character as an arable land weed.

Poa pratensis.

On most of the pastures examined by Armstrong (**1**), this grass was absent, and only in one case was it found by him to reach : per cent. of the total herbage.

Sutton (**19**) expresses the opinion that " it should be service-able in Wales," but the present results give no confirmation to this view.

Only on Area 2, and then only in very small quantity, was it sown, and its highest P.c. fr. on this area was 0·6, while it was not recorded on the area in three out of six examinations. It was not recorded on Areas 1 and 3, but it had a P.c. fr. of 0·1 on Area 4 at $13\frac{1}{2}$ years, and on Area 6 at $5\frac{1}{2}$ years.

On all pastures examined by the writer its highest P.c. fr. was 3·2.[1]

Poa trivialis.

Armstrong's results (**1**) show that the prevalence of this grass varies in some cases from month to month. He found its average range to be from 0·8 to 5·5 per cent. of the total herbage on first-rate old pastures.

Its seed was not sown on any of the present areas, but the grass was recorded in percentage frequencies ranging from 0·9 to 5·6 on Areas 1-4.[2] It was most strongly represented on Area 3, but it was more strongly represented on Area 1 than on Area 2 at corresponding periods. On Area 1 it decreased from $4\frac{1}{2}$ to $5\frac{1}{2}$ years, but on Area 2 it increased almost regularly from $5\frac{1}{2}$ years to $10\frac{1}{2}$ years. The difference between Area 2 at $10\frac{1}{2}$ years and Area 4 at $13\frac{1}{2}$ years is very marked, and suggests that a rapid decrease would follow on Area 2.

On these areas, however, the grass is fairly strongly indigen-ous, but on Areas 6-8, as shown by its absence from Areas 7 and 8, it is not indigenous under natural conditions. Yet it was

[1] Anglesey, an old pasture of good quality at 50 feet.
[2] This grass was not separated from *P. annua* on Area 3 at $8\frac{1}{2}$ years.

recorded on Area 6 at $5\frac{1}{2}$, $6\frac{1}{2}$ and $7\frac{1}{2}$ years in quantities up to 1·6 per cent., but it seems to have been adversely affected by the heavy grazing with sheep and (or) drought in 1918.[1]

Poa annua.

This was generally of little or no importance, but it had the very high P.c. fr. of 8·4 on Area 1 at $4\frac{1}{2}$ years. Probably this was due to the open condition of the young pasture.

Cynosurus cristatus.

Armstrong (1) found this grass to be more abundant on inferior old pastures than on better pastures, but even in first-rate old pastures he found its range to be from 4·4 to 11·3 per cent. of the total herbage. On the best pasture examined by the present writer it had a P.c. fr. of 12·9 at 18 years. It is not known whether it had been sown in this field or not.

The grass is strongly indigenous to Areas 1-4, but exotic to Areas 6-8 under natural conditions. Its seed was not intentionally sown on the farm until 1911, but it was very prominent on Areas 1, 2 and 3 in the pastures which preceded that of the rotation under investigation. It was especially prominent in the hay crop taken from Area 2 in 1905.

Its seed was not included in the seeds-mixtures for Areas 1-4, and since it very rarely occurs as an impurity in other seed samples (8), (11), (14), its occurrence on these areas must be considered as more or less natural.

On Area 1 its development was very weak at $4\frac{1}{2}$ years, but it had increased considerably at $5\frac{1}{2}$ years. Even then, however, its P.c. fr. was much lower than on Area 2 at the corresponding period. On the latter area it had a P.c. fr. of 8·1 at $5\frac{1}{2}$ years, and with a small set back at $8\frac{1}{2}$, it increased regularly from year to year to 14·7 at $10\frac{1}{2}$ years. By this time it had exceeded the P.c. fr. on Area 4 at $13\frac{1}{2}$ years, so that probably on that area there had been a slight decrease. On Area 3 it was considerably less well developed than on Area 2 at corresponding periods, and even showed a decrease from $8\frac{1}{2}$ years to $9\frac{1}{2}$ years.

[1] cf. Stapledon (15).

The soil conditions on all four areas are very similar, but the treatment of the land and the seeds-mixtures were different.   It is difficult to estimate the influence of the seeds-mixture on the development of the grass.   In habit, the grass most closely resembles *Lolium perenne*, but the results for the two grasses are not complementary, although on Area 2 itself, they were very nearly so.   The total for the two grasses on the other areas differ considerably from those for Area 2.

The difference in the treatment of Areas 1, 2 and 3 has already been referred to, but how this could effect the difference is not at all clear.   The grass is not included by Stapledon in his list of arable land weeds,[1] and therefore, presumably, it does not persist bodily through a period of cultivation.   This would also be expected from its caespitose habit.

It has been mentioned that the grass was very plentiful in the hay crop taken from Area 2 in 1905.   As the hay was mown late in the season it is probable that a large quantity of seed was shed in harvesting, and would be ploughed in in the following winter. It is not known how prevalent the grass may be on land investigated for dormant seeds by Brenchley (3), but it is not mentioned by her as having been produced from dormant seeds, so that there is no direct evidence to show that the seeds of the grass are capable of lying dormant in the soil for any appreciable length of time.[2]   At the same time, this is strongly suggested by the present results.

Another factor which may have had considerable effect is the presence of uncultivable land adjoining Areas 2 and 4.   The grass is fairly abundant in the more open spaces of this land, which would therefore afford a convenient centre of seed distribution. Area 2 lies between this uncultivable land and Areas 1 and 3, but the grass is also fairly abundant on hedge banks surrounding these areas.   The seeds are apparently quite unsuited to wind distribu-

[1](17) Table I.
[2] In a few experiments of a similar kind conducted by the writer, no plants of this grass were obtained, although the soil was taken from land where the grass is abundant.

tion, but the areas are open to sheep in winter and early spring, so that they may be the distributing agents.

As shown by Table IV., p. 16a, the grass was not recorded on Area 8, and it is absent from other land adjoining Areas 6 and 7, so that it may be assumed to be naturally exotic to these. Seed was sown on Area 6 at the rate of 1 lb per acre, and the results, as shown by Table IV., are remarkable. The grass decreased considerably from $4\frac{1}{2}$ years to $5\frac{1}{2}$ years, and again decreased somewhat in the following year, but with the heavy grazing with sheep it again increased, so that even at $7\frac{1}{2}$ years it still had a P.c. fr. of 32·0, and was the most prevalent grass.

The effectiveness of the seeding on this area is strikingly shown by a comparison of the results with those for Area 7, where the grass was not sown. On the latter area the grass had a P.c. fr. of 1·3 at $5\frac{1}{2}$ years, but was not recorded at $6\frac{1}{2}$ years. How far the difference in the herbage of the two areas generally may be due to this factor alone, it is not possible to say, but since the soil and general treatment of the two areas were practically identical, the suggestion that this was the controlling factor is very strong. At least, it appears to be a very important factor, and the difference in the herbage of the two areas well illustrates the importance of a suitable seeds-mixture. It also shows how well a plant which may be exotic or at most only very weakly indigenous to land in its neglected state may flourish on such land when properly cultivated and manured.

Anthoxanthum odoratum.

This grass was not recorded by Armstrong on first-rate old pastures, on excellent recent pastures, nor on an extreme type of poor pasture, and only up to 3 per cent. of the total herbage on other pastures (1).

On the best old pasture examined by the present writer it had a P.c. fr. of 4·5, and on the best pasture of all (at 18 years), 3·7.

It is undoubtedly indigenous to all the present areas, as even on Area 8 it formed 0·5 per cent. of the herbage.

The difference in the development of this grass on Areas 1-4, on none of which had it been sown, is even more striking than that of *Cynosurus cristatus*.   At $5\frac{1}{2}$ years its percentage frequency was 2·3 on Area 1 and 18·9 on Area 2, and on the latter area it increased to 21·2 at $6\frac{1}{2}$ years.   There was a great decrease in the following year, but then again it remained practically constant until another sudden decrease occurred at $10\frac{1}{2}$ years, and by this time there was little difference between Area 2 and Area 3 at $9\frac{1}{2}$ years, but the grass had now a considerably lower P.c. fr. than on Area 4 at $13\frac{1}{2}$ years.

The grass probably does not survive a period of cultivation to any great extent either bodily or as dormant seeds (17), (3), but its "seed" is apparently fairly well suited to rapid dispersal both by wind and animals.   Since it occurs in considerable quantity on the uncultivable ground adjoining Areas 2 and 4, this ground probably formed a very effective seed-distributing centre, and this may be the chief cause of its great abundance on Area 2 in the early part of its history.   Areas 1 and 3 were much more remote from this uncultivable land.

A gradual decrease from the high percentage frequencies of Area 2 at $5\frac{1}{2}$ and $6\frac{1}{2}$ years might be expected in subsequent years, but the sudden decrease from 21·2 at $6\frac{1}{2}$ years to 11·3 at $7\frac{1}{2}$ years is difficult to explain.   A dresssing of Basic Slag was applied to the area at 5 years, but this was followed by a slight increase at $5\frac{1}{2}$ years.   The manure may have a slight encouraging effect on the grass itself, but this may be so much greater on other plants as to put this grass at a disadvantage in competition.   This theory is not borne out by other results obtained.[1]

A small amount of seed was included in the seeds-mixture for Area 6, but not in that for Area 7.   The seeding seems to have been very effective, as the grass formed a very much larger proportion of the herbage of the pasture on the former

[1] On Area 6, the grass decreased somewhat in the year immediately following the application of Slag, and increased slightly in the following year. The ultimate effect of Slag on the grass is in some cases at least relatively very small, --- (23).

than on the latter area. Even with this small seeding, however, the grass was much less represented on Area 6 than on
Area 2 up to $6\frac{1}{2}$ years, but at $7\frac{1}{2}$ years it was more developed on
Area 6. The increase on Area 6 at $7\frac{1}{2}$ years seems to indicate
that this grass is encouraged by heavy grazing with sheep, but
during the examinations abundant evidence was found that this
was not due to their neglect of the plant itself.

The behaviour of the grass on these areas suggests that under
these conditions it is not a very strenuous competitor, although it
may recolonise the land rapidly and become very prominent in a
young pasture where a suitable seed-distributing centre is near
at hand. In the absence of such a centre it colonises but slowly,
and in such cases, if the presence of the grass is desired in the
pasture, colonisation on suitable soil may be greatly accelerated
by the inclusion of even a very small quantity of the seed in a
seeds-mixture.

Holcus lanatus.

Armstrong's results (1) show that the presence or absence of
this grass in a pasture is no reliable indication of the quality of
the pasture, but 'results obtained by Hall and Russell (6)[1] seem
to show that on the whole it is more plentiful on the better
feeding pastures.

The seeds of the grass are never intentionally included in
seeds-mixtures, but low grade seed samples of *Lolium* spp.
especially may contain considerable quantities of them (8),
(11), (14).

It was not recorded on Area 8 (grass-heath) nor on Area 7
at $5\frac{1}{2}$ years, and only in very small quantity on the latter area at
$6\frac{1}{2}$ years, but on Area 6 it was fairly well represented except at $5\frac{1}{2}$
years. The cause of its abnormally low proportion in this year as
compared with other years is not known, but it may be a
temporary effect of the Basic Slag which was applied at 4 years.
The manure had no such effect on the grass on Area 2 however,
as on that area there was a continuous increase from 2·5 per cent.

---

[1] These results were obtained by quite a different method of analysis, so
they are rarely referred to in this paper.

at $5\frac{1}{2}$ years to 8·7 per cent. at $9\frac{1}{2}$ years, followed by a decrease to 6·8 per cent. at $10\frac{1}{2}$ years.

The grass was much more abundant on Area 1 than on Area 2 at corresponding periods. On the former area there had been a sudden increase from 4·8 per cent. at $4\frac{1}{2}$ years to 9·3 per cent. at $5\frac{1}{2}$ years. This large and sudden increase may be temporary only, but such a change was not met with on Area 2. The grass seemed to behave differently also on Areas 2 and 3, as on the latter area there was a marked decrease from $8\frac{1}{2}$ to $9\frac{1}{2}$ years. On Area 4, however, its P.c. fr. at $13\frac{1}{2}$ years was very near that for Area 2 at $9\frac{1}{2}$ years.

On the whole, therefore, this grass seems to increase fairly gradually up to about 10 years on this soil, but then acquires a degree of stability. On soil-type i. (Areas 6-8) its developmemt seems to depend very largely on the species it has to compete with. On Area 7, where its chief competitor was *Agrostis tenuis*, it made very little progress up to $6\frac{1}{2}$ years, but on Area 6, where *A. tenuis* was apparently kept well in check by other species, it was more successful.

Agrostis spp.

Only traces of these grasses were found on an extreme type of poor pasture investigated by Armstrong, but on first-rate old pastures he found them in quantities up to 10 per cent. of the total herbage (**1**). On the best pasture investigated by the present writer they had a percentage frequency of 27·1. The highest P.c. fr. found was on a neglected 12 year old pasture, where it reached 92·9 of the total herbage.[1]

Both *A. alba* and *A. tenuis* occur on Areas 1-4, but they were not separated in the examinations. On these areas, they are probably the most troublesome of all arable land weeds, and they are very difficult to eradicate even with the most thorough cleaning. Brenchley (**3**) obtained 43 "seedlings" from the soil from two holes 6in. × 6in. × 9in. in arable land "under ordinary farm management," and they were recorded by Stapledon (**17**) in

[1] Great Orme, Llandudno, 500 feet.

land under Roots, Cereals and Seeds. It is not surprising, therefore, to find the genus strongly represented even in a young pasture, and although a thorough cleaning may have a considerable effect for some years in some cases, the fact that the grasses had a higher P.c. fr. on Area 3 at $9\frac{1}{2}$ years than on Area 2 at the corresponding period suggests that after some lapse of time this has little effect.

The genus was less strongly represented on Area 1 than on Area 2 at corresponding periods, but the difference was not very great. On Area 2, however, there was a considerable decrease from $6\frac{1}{2}$ to $7\frac{1}{2}$ years. This, although there was no apparent change in the season immediately following its application ($6\frac{1}{2}$ years), may be connected with the application of Basic Slag. Between $8\frac{1}{2}$ and $9\frac{1}{2}$ years there was again a large increase, and the P.c. fr. of these grasses was very nearly the same for Area 3 at $9\frac{1}{2}$ years, Area 2 at $9\frac{1}{2}$ years and $10\frac{1}{2}$ years, and Area 4 at $13\frac{1}{2}$ years, but even then the genus was less represented than on the best pasture examined by the writer.

On Areas 6-8 only *Agrostis tenuis* was present. It formed 42·9 per cent. of the total herbage of the old grass-heath (Area 8), but it formed 58·7 per cent. of the total herbage of Area 7 even at $5\frac{1}{2}$ years, and this increased to 69·3 per cent. under heavy grazing at $6\frac{1}{2}$ years. The same influence of very heavy grazing was found on Area 6, where the grass increased from 8·6 per cent. at $6\frac{1}{2}$ years to 27·2 per cent. at $7\frac{1}{2}$ years. On this area the grass had an exceedingly low P.c. fr. at $4\frac{1}{2}$, $5\frac{1}{2}$ and $6\frac{1}{2}$ years in spite of the fact that the area had not been under a cleaning crop.

Since the soil conditions and the general treatment were practically identical for the two areas, the difference in the development of *Agrostis* must apparently be attributed to either of the following two causes :—

(*a*) As already stated, a crop of hay was taken from Area 6 at $1\frac{1}{4}$ years from seeding, while Area 7 was grazed at the corresponding period. Area 6 was, however, put at a disadvantage to the extent that it was not compensated for this extra crop taken by extra manuring, but in spite of this,

Agrostis was incomparably more prevalent on Area 7 in later years.   As Area 7 was grazed with cattle only, at this period, it is not probable that a serious amount of the sown seed-lings would be uprooted.   On the whole, therefore, it does not seem probable that the difference was due to this cause.

(*b*) The seeds-mixtures for the two areas were quite different in some respects, and the   success of *Cynosurus cristatus* especially, and to a smaller extent of *Anthoxanthum odoratum* and *Lolium perenne* on Area 6 seems to indicate that this was the main cause.   The development of *Dactylis glomerata* evidently had no appreciable influence against *Agrostis*, as this was even better developed on Area 7 than on Area 6.

Aira caryophyllea.

This grass is not indigenous to any of the present areas, and it was only recorded once.   It is known to have been present in considerable abundance in the very young pasture of Area 3, to which its seed was probably introduced as an impurity in other grass seeds.[1]

Sieglingia decumbens.

This grass was not recorded on Areas 1-4, but it formed 18·8 per cent. of the herbage of the old grass-heath of Area 8.   It was also found in all examinations of Areas 6 and 7, but on the former area in relatively very small amounts.

LEGUMINOSAE.

In addition to the Percentage Frequency examinations, the areas were examined for these plants by the Specific Frequency method.

Trifolium pratense.

The seeds of a number of so-called varieties of this plant are obtainable commercially, and it has been shown that not only may these varieties differ considerably from each other in some

---

[1] Its seed is a common impurity of *Festuca duriuscula* and *Cynosurus cristatus* seed (8), (11).

respects, but that even plants obtained from seed sold under a similar name, if they have been produced in different countries, may differ in behaviour when grown in this country (12).

At least four of these "varieties" have been used on the farm on which the present areas are situated, and it is very probable that those bought merely as "Broad Red" or "Red" Clover seeds may have had different countries of origin.

Only on Areas 4 and 6 was a single variety sown, so that on the other areas it can not be determined which variety may have left persistent plants.[1] This does not seem to be of very great importance here however, as the results obtained are all very low.

Traces were recorded by the percentage frequency method on Area 2 at $6\frac{1}{2}$ and $7\frac{1}{2}$ years, on Area 3 at $8\frac{1}{2}$ years, and on Area 6 at $5\frac{1}{3}$ years, while on Area 6 also a P.c. fr. of 0·1 was recorded at $4\frac{1}{2}$ years. The only other P.c. fr. result was 0·4 per cent. on Area 4 at $13\frac{1}{2}$ years.

The Specific Frequency results are more definite, although relatively few were obtained. After a seeding of "Broad Red" and "Cowgrass" a Sp. fr. of 19 was obtained on Area 1 at $3\frac{1}{2}$ years, and a Sp. fr. of 1 at $4\frac{1}{2}$ years. With a heavier seeding, but of a similar kind, the plant was not recorded on Area 2 at $5\frac{1}{2}$ years, but it had sp. frequencies of 2 and 3 at $8\frac{1}{2}$ years and $10\frac{1}{2}$ years repectively, while a relatively light seeding of "Broad Red" and "Hybrid Cow Clover" gave a Sp. fr. of 2 on Area 3 at $7\frac{1}{2}$ years, and the same Sp. fr. was obtained on Area 5 at $10\frac{1}{2}$ years with a heavy seeding of "Broad Red" and "Cowgrass." A Sp. fr. of 6 was found on Area 4 at $13\frac{1}{2}$ years.

From these results it appears that under these conditions the development of the plant has two distinct periods. It decreases rapidly from sowing, so that at $4\frac{1}{2}$ or $5\frac{1}{2}$ years it has practically if not quite disappeared. After this, it seems to increase slowly up to $13\frac{1}{2}$ years at least.

It seems very probable that the second period of develop-

---

[1] These "varieties" can not be separated by botanical characters from each other, nor from the indigenous plants, in the vegetative state.

ment is due to recolonisation by the indigenous variety, but this has not been proved.[1]

The plant is probably completely exotic to Areas 6-8. "Cowgrass" was sown on Area 6 and on Area 7 at the rate of 2lb. per acre, and on the latter area 2lb. per acre "Late-flowering Red Clover" seed was also sown.

On Area 6, the plant was recorded in the P.c. fr. examinations at $4\frac{1}{2}$ and at $5\frac{1}{2}$ years, but its development was very small, as at $5\frac{1}{2}$ years it had only a Sp. fr. of 2. On Area 7, however, it had a Sp. fr. of 10 at $4\frac{1}{2}$ years, so that in this situation, either owing to the conditions or treatment or owing to the difference in the varieties of seeds sown, it has persisted to a greater extent than on Area 1.

Trifolium hybridum.

This plant is not indigenous to any of the areas, but its seed was included in the seeds-mixtures for all except Area 8 and possibly Area 4.

The results obtained show that its persisting powers are generally small under some conditions. It was not recorded on Areas 1-4 by the P.c. fr. method, and only to the extent of a Sp. fr. of 2 on Area 1 at $3\frac{1}{2}$ years by the other method.

On Area 7 it was not recorded by either method, but on Area 6 it was much more successful, as on the latter area it was recorded by the P.c. fr. method at $4\frac{1}{2}$, $5\frac{1}{2}$ and $6\frac{1}{2}$ years, but not at $7\frac{1}{2}$ years, and it also had a Sp. fr. of 15 at $5\frac{1}{2}$ years.

On Area 6, the plant did remarkably well throughout. It produced a relatively large amount of herbage up to the fourth year, but no determinations were made before $4\frac{1}{2}$ years. In the third summer it produced ripe seeds quite freely in tufts surrounding cattle droppings, and it is possible that its relatively long persistence on this area is largely due to this. In whatever way it did persist, it did so on this area to a much greater extent than *Trifolium pratense*, but on Area 7 it was much less successful than the latter plant.

[1] On an old pasture field on the farm, a remarkable development of the indigenous variety followed the application of Basic Slag.

Here again probably we see the effect of the other constituents of the seeds-mixtures, as the seeds of this plant were included in equal quantities for the two areas.

Trifolium repens.

On an oat stubble following ley, the present writer has found a Sp. fr. of 18 for this plant,[1] but it is not included in a list of arable land weeds given by Stapledon (17). Brenchley (3) obtained 131 seedlings of this plant from the soil from four holes (6in. × 6in. × 9in) in a field which had been under grass for some years.

The present writer collected ripe seed in 1916, and in April, 1917, a portion of these were treated with fine emery paper. These, and others which had not been treated, were then placed under similar germinating conditions, and the following germination results were obtained :—

	10 days.	25 days.	2 mths.	4 mths.	6 mths.	8 mths.
Treated	66[2]	77	83	85	86	86[3]
Untreated	7	7	7	10	10	12

At the end of eight months the test on the treated seeds was discontinued, and the untreated seeds were allowed to dry gradually, and to remain in the dry condition for four months. At the end of this time there were 81 per cent. hard[4] seeds left, while 7 per cent. had become mouldy.

The hard seeds were then collected and treated with emery paper, but in this process a further 7 per cent. of the original number were lost, leaving 74 per cent. for further testing.

In three days, 48 per cent. of the original number had germinated normally, and 5 per cent. abnormally.[5] The test was

[1] Anglesey, poor soil at 150 feet.

[2] Numbers in percentages of total seeds tested.

[3] Some seeds had probably escaped treatment.

[4] *i.e.* seeds which appear normal and healthy although they have not germinated under conditions which produce rapid germination of other apparently similar seeds.

[5] This was probably due to the emery paper treatment.

allowed to run for five months, and in the meantime a further 25 per cent. germinated normally, leaving only 1 per cent. which was still " hard."

Thus seeds which were capable of immediate germination, provided their coats were made permeable to water, remained dormant for eight months under conditions which in other seeds produced rapid germination, and after being allowed to dry for four months were still capable of normal germination after treatment with emery paper.

All these results leave little room for doubt that dead ripe seeds of this plant may remain dormant in the soil for a very long period, and still be capable of producing normal seedlings when by some means their coats are rendered permeable.[1] It is to be expected therefore that where a pasture field in which there is a fair development of the plant is brought under cultivation, the plant may appear in the subsequent pasture in some quantity although no seed be sown.

The seed of at least two varieties of this plant are obtainable commercially. These are known as " White or Dutch Clover" (*Trifolium repens*) and " Wild White Clover " (*T. repens*, var. *silvestre*), (7), (20).[2] The value of these two varieties of seeds in the formation of a pasture has been examined by the writer, and the results published elsewhere (9). These results showed that on an average, with the same weight of seed, at $2\frac{1}{2}$ years from sowing, 19·7 per cent. of the ground on which " Wild White Clover " seed had been sown was covered by the plant, as compared with 2·13 per cent. of the ground on which " White or Dutch " seed had been sown.

[1] The conditions of the experiment are in some ways different from those which occur in the soil. It is possible that soil water has a different effect from tap water. Soil organisms (except animals) are not likely to have any effect on them as the hard seeds of the experiment were quite immune from the attacks of fungi.

[2] It is difficult to understand why the wild form shonld be regarded by seedsmen as the variety, as it is very much more probable that the " Dutch " is the variety, produced by continued cultivation and unconscious selection of the wild form.

In an experiment on the College Farm, Bangor, the following results were obtained :—

Variety of seed :	Dutch	Dutch	Wild	None
lb. of seed per acre :	2	1	1	—
Sp. fr. at $1\frac{1}{2}$ years :	91	98	99	85
Sp. fr. at 2 years :	97	100	100	86

These results are inconclusive as between the two varieties, but they show clearly that even without seeding the plant may be well distributed in a young pasture.

The Specific Frequency method is generally unsatisfactory as a means of comparing the development of this plant, as even where not strongly represented it may give the maximum Sp. fr. This is clearly shown by the results for Area 2, where the plant had a Sp. fr. of 100 and a P.c. fr. of 12·4 at $5\frac{1}{2}$ years, and a Sp. fr. of 98 and a P.c. fr. of 18·2 at $8\frac{1}{2}$ years. For this reason, the P.c. fr. results chiefly will be made use of.

" White or Dutch " seed was sown on Areas 1, 2, 3, 6 and 7, but not on the other areas. That the prevalence of the plant in the ensuing pasture at $5\frac{1}{2}$ years does not depend on the amount of this seed sown is clearly shown by the results for Areas 1 and 2. At this date the plant had a P.c. fr. of 31·8 on Area 1, where only $\frac{1}{2}$lb. per acre had been sown, while it had only a P.c. fr. of 12·4 on Area 2 from 2lb. seed per acre. Since the soil, altitude, and grazing are similar on the two areas the cause of this difference must be sought elsewhere. It may partly be due to the difference in the other components of the seeds-mixtures, but this does not seem probable. It may also be due to the high development of *Cynosurus cristatus* and *Anthoxanthum odoratum* on Area 2. The most probable cause, however, is the difference in treatment —partly the treatment while under cultivation, and partly the subsequent treatment, and especially that Area 2 was given a dressing of farmyard manure after one hay crop had been taken, while Area 2 was not manured until the winter following this examination.[1]

[1] It is believed also that the phosphatic manure applied to Area 1 when sown down to grass was Basic Slag, while Superphosphate was used for Area 2.

The sudden increase of the plant on Area 2 at $6\frac{1}{2}$ years was undoubtedly due to the application of Basic Slag (16), (13), but the effect of the Slag was not very lasting here, as at $8\frac{1}{2}$ years the plant was almost equally well developed on Area 3, which had not been slagged. On this latter area, however, the relatively high development of the plant may be due to the thorough cleaning of the land, but at $9\frac{1}{2}$ years it was only slightly more abundant on Area 2 than on Area 4 at $13\frac{1}{2}$ years, which had not been slagged, and on which the plant had not been sown, so that apparently the effect of the Slag on this plant was exhausted in three years.

The plant was not recorded by either method of examination on Area 8, but it is known that weak plants were to be found in the former grass heath of Area 6. "White or Dutch" seed was sown on Areas 6 and 7, but the plant had a P.c. fr. of only 8·4 on the former area at $4\frac{1}{2}$ years. Following a dressing of Basic Slag, however, it increased to 27·3 in the following year, and at $6\frac{1}{2}$ years it still had a P.c. fr. 24·7. Its decrease was then as rapid as its previous increase, probably to a great extent owing to the exhaustion of the effect of the Slag, but partly also probably to the effect of the drought.[1] The same quantity of seed was sown on Area 7, but this area was not examined by the P.c. fr. at $4\frac{1}{2}$ years. The Sp. fr. of the plant at that date was relatively low (sp. fr. = 60). and its P.c. fr. at $5\frac{1}{2}$ years, following a dressing of Basic Slag as on Area 6, at the corresponding date, was very much lower than on the latter area, so that here again apparently the effect of the seeds-mixture as a whole is seen.

From these results it is seen that the amount of "White or Dutch" seed sown may bear no relationship to the development of the plant at $5\frac{1}{2}$ years, and that at $13\frac{1}{2}$ years at most, its inclusion has no apparent effect on some soils. Its development in the pasture appears to be very largely a matter of cultivation, manuring and treatment, but other results (9) show that "Wild White Clover" seed may hasten the development of the plant very considerably in a pasture.

[1] It has been found elsewhere that heavy grazing with sheep has no such effect on the plant. Cf. Stapledon on the effect of drought (15).

Anthyllis Vulneraria.

This plant is not indigenous to this farm, but, as shown by Table I., the seed has often been included in seeds-mixtures in recent years. It was first introduced on Area 2 in 1908, but at the rate of only $\frac{1}{4}$lb. per acre. On this area rare plants were to be found up to $2\frac{1}{2}$ years, but on Areas 1 and 2, where it was also sown, it was not found after $1\frac{1}{2}$ years.

On Area 6, it gave remarkable results in the hay crop at $1\frac{1}{4}$ years from a seeding of 2lb. per acre, but it had almost completely disappeared at $2\frac{1}{2}$ years except on the thinnest soil, and even here it was not recorded in P.c. fr. examinations at $4\frac{1}{2}$ years and subsequently, nor in the Sp. fr. examination at $5\frac{1}{2}$ years. It also developed fairly well up to $1\frac{1}{2}$ years on Area 7, but it then disappeared, and was not recorded in the detailed examinations of this area.

Medicago sativa (Exotic).

This was sown on Areas 6 and 7, but it made a very poor development, and was not recorded in the examinations.

Medicago lupulina (Exotic).

This was sown on Area 5, but was not recorded in the Sp. fr. examination at $10\frac{1}{2}$ years.

Trifolium dubium (Not sown).

The seed of this plant has never been intentionally sown on the farm, but it often occurs as an impurity in seed samples of *Trifolium repens* and *T. hybridum* (8), (11). The plant is sometimes plentiful in a well-manured permanent hay field on the farm, but otherwise it is not very noticeable.

On the present areas its highest P.c. fr. was 2·6 on Area 6 at $6\frac{1}{2}$ years, but by the following year its P.c. fr. on this area was only 0·9. Its highest Sp. fr. was 4 on Area 1 at $4\frac{1}{2}$ years, and on Area 6 at $5\frac{1}{2}$ years.

Lathyrus sp. (Not sown).

Traces of this genus were found on Area 2 at $6\frac{1}{2}$, $7\frac{1}{2}$, $8\frac{1}{2}$ and $9\frac{1}{2}$ years, but it was not otherwise recorded.

Lotus spp. (Not sown).

L. corniculatus was the only species recorded on Areas 6-8, but traces of *L. uliginosus* were also found on Areas 1-5. The two species were not separated in these examinations.

The Percentage Frequency method of examination is not very satisfactory on young pastures for these plants owing to their habit of frequently occurring in colonies. The Sp. fr. method is probably more reliable, as the plant seldom reaches a high Sp. fr., and therefore its relative distribution is a good guide to comparison. The results obtained by the P.c. fr. method are however given in Table V., p. 16*b*.

The highest P.c. fr. for Areas 1-4 was 0·8 on Area 2 at $9\frac{1}{2}$ years, and on Area 4 at $13\frac{1}{2}$ years.

The genus was not recorded on Area 1 by the Sp. fr. method, but the other records for these areas ranged from a Sp. fr. of 2 on Area 3 at $7\frac{1}{2}$ years, to 37 on Area 4 at $13\frac{1}{2}$ years. The results for Area 2 are irregular, as the Sp. fr. was lower at $8\frac{1}{2}$ years than at $5\frac{1}{2}$ years, but it was higher at $10\frac{1}{2}$ years than at $5\frac{1}{2}$ years. On this area, therefore, there appeared on the whole to be a tendency to increase, but not to the same extent as on Area 4. The difference between Areas 1, 2, 3 and 5 are capable of explanation by reference to the treatment of the land while under cultivation, together with the assumption that the tendency to increase is real on these areas, as Area 2 was not under a cleaning crop. But the high Sp. fr. on Area 4 is difficult to explain as this area was also partly under a cleaning crop. This area had not been manured, however, since it was laid down to grass, but Basic Slag does not usually depress these plants (23). It may be that the difference between Areas 2 and 4 is merely an indication that in the later history of a young pasture these plants develop very rapidly.

The highest P.c. fr. and the highest Sp. fr. were obtained on the old grass-heath (Area 8). On both Area 6 and Area 7 the P.c. fr. results indicate a decrease with an increase in the age of the pasture. It is very probable that this plant is capable of surviving cultivation bodily,[1] and that on Area 6 especially it was less suitable for the new conditions created, and therefore suffered in competition with other plants. The Sp. fr. for the plant on this area at $5\frac{1}{2}$ years was very low considering that the area had not been under a cleaning crop, and the difference between this and the Sp. fr. for Area 7 at $4\frac{1}{2}$ years is very marked. In respect of this plant, Area 7 was again reverting much more rapidly than Area 6 towards the grass-heath condition of Area 8.

OTHER ORDERS.*

The plant unit in most of the species included under this heading is relatively large,[2] and as they rarely form a very large proportion of the herbage the P.c. fr. results are generally low. In most cases, therefore, the Sp. fr. method is more satisfactory, and the discussion of these species will be mainly based on the Specific Frequency results.

Results were obtained for a few species which are not included in the tables owing to the fact that their development was very small. Some of these were sown species.

Cichorium Intybus (Exotic).

The seeds of this plant were included in the seeds-mixtures for Areas 6 and 7 at the rate of 2lb. per acre.

It had a P.c. fr. of 0·1 on Area 6 at $4\frac{1}{2}$ years, but otherwise was not recorded by this method. It had Sp. fr. of 3 and 2 on Areas 6 and 7 at $5\frac{1}{2}$ and $4\frac{1}{2}$ years respectively, so that although not indigenous, it had persisted to some extent for over five years.

Poterium Sanguisorba (Exotic).

This was sown on Areas 6 and 7 at the rate of 3lb. per acre. It was not recorded in the P.c. fr. examinations, but it had Sp. frequencies of 3 and 2 respectively on these areas, the former area examined at $5\frac{1}{2}$ years and the latter at $4\frac{1}{2}$ years.

---

[1] This is suggested by a comparison of Areas 2 and 3.
*See Table V., p. 16b.
[2] Definition i., p. 1.

Carum Petroselinum (Exotic).

This was also sown on Areas 6 and 7 at the rate of 2lb. per acre, but the plant was not recorded in the examinations.

Plantago lanceolata.

The seed of this plant has often been included in seeds-mixtures on this farm (Table I., p. 4), and it was included in those for Areas 3, 5 and 7, and also probably in that for Area 4. Its seed is also often found in samples of *Trifolium pratense* seed (8), (11), (14), so that probably a small amount would be introduced in this way.

Its Sp. fr. was quite low on Area 1 both at $3\frac{1}{2}$ and at $4\frac{1}{2}$ years, and in spite of the fact that it had been sown on Area 3 its Sp. fr. was considerably lower on this area than on Area 2, where it had not been sown. On Area 5, where also it had been sown, its Sp. fr. was only 23 at $10\frac{1}{2}$ years, as compared with 27 on Area 2 at the corresponding period. Its extreme development, however, was on Area 4, where it had a Sp. fr. of 81 at $13\frac{1}{2}$ years.

Stapledon found this plant to occur in some quantity as an arable land weed, and in considerable abundance in pastures of less than a year old ("seeds") (17), but Brenchley found its seeds quite unimportant amongst buried weed seeds (3). It is quite possible, therefore, that the relative abundance of the plant on Area 2 is due to the imperfect cleaning given to the land. It is surprising, however, to find that the seed sown had been relatively so ineffective on Areas 3 and 5.

On Area 7 a seeding of 3lb. per acre was considerably more effective, as here there was a Sp. fr. of 26 at $4\frac{1}{2}$ years as compared with a Sp. fr. of 6 on Area 6 at $5\frac{1}{2}$ years, where the seed had not been sown. As shown by a Sp. fr. of 10 for Area 8 (old grass-heath), the plant was more or less indigenous to these areas.[1]

Achillea Millefolium.

The seed of this plant was not sown on any of the present areas, and it had not been sown on the farm until some time after these areas had been laid down to grass. It is not included by

[1] On Area 8 it was chiefly found along sheep tracks.

Stapledon in his list of arable land weeds (**17**), and Brenchley shows that its seeds rarely lie dormant except in the soils of very old grass land (**3**). It was not recorded by the present writer on an oat stubble, and the following results obtained on well cleaned land[1] at 50 feet also show that the plant may not occur where not sown :—

Seed sown in lb. per acre :	o	$\frac{1}{8}$	$\frac{1}{4}$	$\frac{1}{2}$
Sp. fr. at $1\frac{1}{2}$ years :	o	9	23	27
,, 2 ,, :	o	14·5	33·5	35

On the other hand, the following results obtained on imperfectly cleaned land,[2] show that it may occur in some quantity even in young pastures, and that in some such cases the inclusion of seed in the seeds-mixture may have no appreciable effect :—

Seed sown in lb. per acre :	nil	$\frac{1}{4}$
Sp. fr. at $1\frac{1}{2}$ years :	6	4
,, ,, 2 ,,	2	8
,, ,, $2\frac{1}{2}$,,	8	8

On the whole, these results tend to show that the plant does not usually persist through a period of cultivation which includes a cleaning crop, but that where the land is imperfectly cleaned, especially at relatively high elevations, it may persist by some means. Its obvious success, at least in some cases, when sown on well-cleaned land, shows that although it may not appear spontaneously in the young pasture, the conditions in those cases are not such as to inhibit its growth.

In view of this, the results for Areas 1-8 are especially interesting. The plant had a Sp. fr. of 10 on the old grass-heath (Area 8), but it was not recorded on Area 7 at $4\frac{1}{2}$ years, nor on Area 6 at $5\frac{1}{2}$ years. In this case, therefore, it had been completely

---

[1] These are average results for four plots each over three acres in extent, and six plots each a fourth of an acre in extent, all in the same field, at the College Farm, Aber, Bangor.

[2] Penmachno, 775 feet. The two areas are the two halves of the same field.

eradicated, although no cleaning crop had been taken. On Area 1, which had been partly under a cleaning crop, it had a Sp. fr. of only 2 both at $3\frac{1}{2}$ years and at $4\frac{1}{2}$ years. It is rather surprising, therefore, to find that on Area 3, which had been entirely under a cleaning crop, it had a Sp. fr. of 41 at $7\frac{1}{2}$ years. In fact, it was probably only slightly less prevalent on this area than on Area 2, which had not been even partly under a cleaning crop. The development of the plant on Area 2 was, however, very rapid. There is a very marked difference between this area at $5\frac{1}{2}$ years and Area 1 at $4\frac{1}{2}$ years, but this would naturally be assumed to be due to the difference in cultivation were it not for the results for Area 3, and the results for Areas 4 and 5 would not contradict this conclusion as each of these had been partly under a cleaning crop.

If we assumed that for some unknown reason[1] the development of the plant on Area 3 was abnormal, the other results would be straight-forward. They would show that under the conditions prevailing for Areas 1-5 the plant is strongly indigenous, and that although the land may be put partly under a cleaning crop the plant may be very prevalent on relatively young pastures, but that where the land is not even partly put under a cleaning crop its development is very rapid, its Sp. fr. rising from 39 at $5\frac{1}{2}$ years to 76 at $10\frac{1}{2}$ years.

On Area 3, however, the effect of a thorough cleaning was exceedingly small.

Under the conditions prevailing on Areas 6-8 on the other hand, its appearance may be delayed very considerably even though the land is not put under a cleaning crop.

Other results mentioned show that in some cases at least the inclusion of the seed in the seeds-mixture may be very effective where the land is thoroughly cleaned, and that with low quantities of seed, the distribution of the plant in the young pasture bears a definite relationship to the amount of seed sown. In some cases, however, the inclusion of the seed may be ineffective.

---

[1] The seed of the plant never occurs in any appreciable quantity in other seed samples (8), (11), (14).

Ranunculus repens.[1]

Stapledon found this plant to be one of the most important arable land weeds (17), and Brenchley classifies it amongst "arable or grass land plants" (3).

It was not recorded on Area 8 (old grass-heath), but it was recorded on all the other areas by both methods of examination. On Areas 6 and 7 it was, however, much less important than on most of the other areas.

The P.c. fr. results for Areas 1-4 on the whole indicate that it is most prevalent in the young pasture under the prevailing conditions, and that it decreases with the increasing age of the pasture. The results for Area 3, however, are very high as compared with those for Area 2 at corresponding periods.

This greater development of the plant on Area 3 is also apparently indicated by the Sp. fr. results, as on this area the plant had a Sp. fr. of 78 at $7\frac{1}{2}$ years, as compared with a Sp. fr. of 62 on Area 2 at $8\frac{1}{2}$ years. The latter result may be slightly abnormal however, as on the same area there was a Sp. fr. of 70 at $10\frac{1}{2}$ years.

The Sp. fr. results for Areas 1-5 as a whole seem to indicate that the plant increases up to $4\frac{1}{2}$ or $5\frac{1}{2}$ years, and then decreases fairly rapidly. The very low Sp. fr. on Area 4 may be due to competition with other plants, especially *Plantago lanceolata*, which had a very high Sp. fr. on this area. If anything, these results tend to show that a thorough cleaning of the land is favourable to the development of the plant, but there is little to show to what extent it is affected by the composition of the seeds-mixture used.

Bellis perennis.

This plant may also occur in considerable quantity as an arable land weed (17).

It was not recorded on Area 8, and its development on

---

[1] The seeds of the remaining plants are never intentionally included in seeds-mixtures, but those of some of them are frequently found in other seed samples (8), (11), (14).

Areas 6 and 7 was relatively very small, as on these areas its highest Sp. fr. was 18 on Area 6 at $5\frac{1}{2}$ years.

It was, however, very widely distributed on the other areas, and gave considerably higher P.c. fr. results than *Ranunculus repens*.

The results for Areas 1, 2, 4 and 5 are, on the whole, fairly regular, and from these it would appear that the plant increases up to $5\frac{1}{2}$ years or perhaps even somewhat later, but then decreases fairly rapidly. The results for Area 3 are different, and they show that the plant may have a Sp. fr. very little short of the maximum even at $7\frac{1}{2}$ years, and a very high P.c. fr. at $9\frac{1}{2}$ years. It is difficult to find any cause for this difference except that Area 3 had been more thoroughly cleaned than the other areas while under cultivation.

Prunella vulgaris.

This is regarded by Brenchley as a grass land plant (3), but Stapledon found it to occur frequently as an arable land weed, and especially in pastures less than a year old (17). Its seed is fairly frequently found in other seed samples, especially in those of *Trifolium hybridum* and *T. repens* (8), (11), (14).

It had a Sp. fr. of 7 even on Area 8 (grass-heath), but on Area 6, at $5\frac{1}{2}$ years, it had a Sp. fr. of 54, while on Area 7 (which has been found to be approaching the grass-heath condition at a more rapid rate than Area 6 in other respects) it had only a Sp. fr. of 22 at $4\frac{1}{2}$ years.

On Areas 1, 2, 4 and 5 the results are again fairly regular, showing a maximum development at about $5\frac{1}{2}$ years. The Sp. fr. results for Area 3 agree fairly well with the others, but the P.c. fr. results for this area and for Area 4 are abnormally high.[1]

Cerastium vulgatum.

This plant was recorded in all examinations except on Area 8, but its development was small on other areas. On Areas

---

[1] These areas were all examined, August - September in each year, and at this time there are usually a fairly large number of seedlings of this plant. The P.c. fr. results, therefore, depend very largely on the number of seedlings produced.

1-4 it was much more widely distributed, and had a much higher P.c. fr. up to $5\frac{1}{2}$ years than later. Different from species already mentioned, this plant decreased very rapidly in most cases, so that on Area 2 its Sp. fr. had decreased from 67 at $5\frac{1}{2}$ years to 4 at $8\frac{1}{2}$ years. Its Sp. fr. on Area 5 at $10\frac{1}{2}$ years was relatively very high as compared with the other areas. This may be due to the slightly lighter soil.[1]

Sagina procumbens.

Owing to the habit of this plant, it is not easy to detect it where the turf is fairly thick and the plants small, so that the P.c. fr. results may be more reliable than those obtained by the Sp. fr. method.

The highest P.c. fr. was obtained on Area 2 at $7\frac{1}{2}$ years, and apparently, on Areas 1-5 it reached its maximum at about this time, and then decreased fairly rapidly.

It was not recorded on Area 8, and on Areas 6 and 7 it was but poorly represented except on Area 6 at $6\frac{1}{2}$ years. In respect of this plant Area 6 appeared to be reverting to the heath condition more rapidly than Area 7.

Luzula campestris.

Few records were obtained for this plant by the Sp. fr. method. Its highest P.c. fr. was obtained on Area 8 (grass-heath), but as compared with other areas, especially Area 6, at the corresponding periods, it was well represented on Area 7 both at $5\frac{1}{2}$ and $6\frac{1}{2}$ years. Only traces were recorded on Area 6, so that in respect of this plant Area 7 was reverting to heath condition most rapidly.

The plant was not recorded on Area 1 at $4\frac{1}{2}$ years nor on Area 3 at $8\frac{1}{2}$ years, and it was but poorly represented on these areas a year later in each case.

The results for the other areas seem to show that on this land it tends to increase with the increasing age of the pasture, although its P.c. fr. was lower at $10\frac{1}{2}$ years than at $9\frac{1}{2}$

[1] On old pastures examined by the writer, its highest P.c. fr. was 1·3 on a soil inclined to be gravelly or sandy (College Farm, Bangor).

years on Area 2, as on Area 4 at 13½ years it had a very high percentage frequency.

Potentilla erecta.

As shown by a Sp. fr. of 87 on Area 8, this is a typical grass-heath plant.[1] It is recorded as an abundant arable land weed in exceptional cases by Stapledon (17), and results obtained by the present writer on land which had been brought under cultivation from a rough grass heath at an elevation of 150 feet in Anglesey,[2] shows that where the land is not thoroughly cleaned it may occur in considerable quantity both in the stubble and in the young pastures. These results were as follows:—

(1) Sp. fr. on pasture		1½ years old :	66
(2) ,,	,,	2½ ,,	46
(3) ,,	,,	2½ ,,	60
(4) ,,	stubble following (3)		46

In these cases, the plants have in most cases undoubtedly survived the period of cultivation bodily, as shown by their strong root-stocks. It is not surprising, therefore, to find the plant fairly widely distributed in most of the present areas.

On Area 1 it was not recorded except in very small quantity at 3½ years, and on Area 3, which had been thoroughly cleaned, it was not recorded in the Sp. fr. examination at 7½ years, and only to a very slight extent by the P.c. fr. method at 9½ years. Even on Area 2, which had not been partly under a cleaning crop, it only had a Sp. fr. of 3 at 5½ years, but this had increased to 17 at 8½ years, and the same Sp. fr. was again found at 10½ years, while on Area 4 adjoining, its Sp. fr. was also 17 at 13½ years. On Area 5 at 10½ years, however, it was much less widely distributed.

Thus, on this type, the plant probably survives a period of imperfect cultivation to some extent, and then increases fairly slowly, but its rate of increase becomes much less when it has attained a Sp. fr. of about 17, and therefore in respect of this

[1] cf. (21).
[2] Ceidio 'Isaf, Llanerchymedd,

plant these conditions do not immediately produce the typical grass-heath.

On Areas 6 and 7 the increase of the plant was much more rapid, but in this case again Area 7 was reverting to the grass-heath type much more rapidly than Area 6.

Leontodon autumnalis.

This plant is obviously not a grass-heath plant as it was not recorded on Areas 7 and 8, and only in minute quantities on Area 6.

It was of frequent occurrence on Areas 1-5, and on Area 4 it reached a Sp. fr. of 65 at $13\frac{1}{2}$ years. On Areas 3 and 5 its increase was less rapid than on Area 2.[1] On the whole it would seem that the plant is capable of surviving a period of imperfect cultivation, and that under the conditions prevailing, its distribution in the pasture extends with the age of the pasture.

Senecio Jacobaea.

The development of this plant in a pasture is usually interfered with by cutting, or sometimes by grazing with sheep. It never flourishes where sheep graze during the summer.

It was of frequent occurrence on most of the present areas, but its development had in most cases been interfered with. On Area 5 for instance, it was not recorded, although it is known to have been present in some quantity before the area was grazed with both cattle and sheep during the summer. Up till 1918 Areas 6 and 7 were only grazed by sheep in the spring, so that the development of the plant had been little interfered with. The plant was recorded at each examination—reaching a Sp. fr. of 18 at $5\frac{1}{2}$ years—on Area 6, but it was not recorded on Area 7, so that in respect of this plant again Area 7 was nearer the heath type than Area 6.

Areas 2 and 3, since they were parts of the same field, were also subject to the same grazing conditions, but here the plant was obviously much more prevalent on Area 3 than on Area 2.

[1] In the Sp. fr. of this area at $5\frac{1}{2}$ years the plant was confused with *Taraxacum vulgare,* so that the results are not given in Table V., p. 16b.

This may be connected with the different treatment given to the two areas while under cultivation.

Rumex Acetosa.

This was not recorded on Areas 6, 7 and 8, and only in small quantities on the other areas. It seems to be most prevalent on the young pastures, but the highest Sp. fr. occurred on Area 5 at $10\frac{1}{2}$ years. This is interesting in view of the fact that this was the only area recently limed, as it is generally understood that " lime applications tend to check its growth " (5).

Centaurea nigra.

This plant is recorded by Stapledon as an arable land weed at high elevations in Mid-Wales (17), and it is likely that where it is fairly strongly indigenous it may survive a period of imperfect cultivation, as the writer has found it to have specific frequencies of 4, 8 and 8 at $1\frac{1}{4}$, 2 and $2\frac{1}{2}$ years respectively under such conditions.[1]

It was not recorded on Area 8, and only in minute quantities on Areas 6 and 7, but on the other areas it was more plentiful. The effect of thorough cleaning of the land is probably seen in the relatively low Sp. fr. of 7 on Area 3 at $7\frac{1}{2}$ years as compared with specific frequencies of 14 and 20 at $8\frac{1}{2}$ and $10\frac{1}{2}$ years respectively on Area 2. It had but a low Sp. fr. on Area 5 at $10\frac{1}{2}$ years, but it is generally believed that it is kept in check by grazing with sheep. Is is obviously a more important constituent of the herbage of the older than the younger pastures under the conditions prevailing for Areas 1-5.

Plantago major.

This was but poorly represented, but it is shown to be at its highest development on the younger pastures.

Rumex Acetosella.

Although not recorded on Area 8, this plant had high specific frequencies on Areas 6 and 7. On these areas, it was a troublesome weed while the land was under cultivation, but the P.c. fr.

[1] Penmachno, 775 feet.

results show that it was decreasing in the pasture. This decrease had not proceeded very far on Area 7 at 4½ years, but the plant was less widely distributed on Area 6 at 5½ years.

Except on Area 1, where it had specific frequencies of 7 and 10 at 3½ and at 4½ years respectively, the plant was rarely recorded on the other areas.

Potentilla anserina.

This was chiefly met with on Area 2, where its maximum Sp. fr. was 24 at 8½ years. This seems to be abnormally high, as on the same area its Sp. fr. was 8 and 9 at 5½ and 10½ years respectively.

It was not recorded on the slightly lighter soils of Areas 5, 6, 7 and 8.

Taraxacum vulgare.

Traces of this plant were found on Area 6 at 7½ years, but otherwise it was not recorded on Areas 6, 7 and 8. Its chief development was on Areas 2 and 4, and on Areas 1-4 its Sp. fr. seemed to be increasing with the age of the pasture.

Chrysanthemum Leucanthemum.—This was chiefly recorded on Area 2, and it appeared to be decreasing with the increased age of the pasture.

Polygala vulgaris.—This plant was recorded in minute quantities on Area 2 at 7½ years and later, and on Area 4 at 13½ years, but otherwise it was not recorded except to a small extent on Area 6 at 5½ years, and on Area 8, where it had a Sp. fr. of 10. It is obviously a plant of the older pastures and the grass-heath.

Veronica officinalis.—This was also recorded on Area 2 in minute quantities at 8½ years and later, and also on Area 4. It had a Sp. fr. of 22 on Area 8, and it was represented on Areas 6 and 7. On these areas, it seems to come in sooner than *Polygala vulgaris*, but it is primarily a grass-heath plant.

Viola canina.—This is also a grass-heath plant, but it was recorded on Area 2 at $8\frac{1}{2}$ years (Sp. fr. = 1).   It had a high Sp. fr. on Area 8, but it was not recorded on Areas 6 and 7.

Hieracium Pilosella was recorded on Areas 3, 6, 7 and 8, but on the former three areas in very small quantities.

Euphrasia officinalis was only recorded on Areas 4 and 8, and it had a considerably higher Sp. fr. on the former than on the latter area.

Thymus Serpyllum.—This grass-heath plant had a Sp. fr. of 55 and a P.c. fr. of 4·2 on Area 8, and minute quantities were found on Areas 6 and 7.

Galium hercynicum is another typical grass-heath plant, and it was recolonising Area 7 at a more rapid rate than most of these plants, but it was recolonising Area 6 much more slowly.

Calluna vulgaris had a fairly wide distribution on Area 8, although, as shown by the P.c. fr. results, it formed but a very small proportion of the total herbage.   It was also recorded on Areas 6 and 7, but its Sp. fr. was small.

The following species were also recorded, but in very small quantities :—

Hypochoeris radicata (Areas 1, 2, 6, 7), *Veronica serpyllifolia* (Areas 2, 3, 5),   *V. Chamaedrys* (Areas 1, 3, 5, 7), *Centaurium umbellatum* (Areas 1, 2), *Ulex europaeus* (Area 8), *Vaccinium Myrtillus* (Areas 6, 8), *Mentha* sp. (Areas 1, 2, 3), *Pteris aquilina*, *Anagallis arvensis* (Area 2), *Hypericum humifusum* (Areas 7, 8),[1] *Cirsium arvense* (Areas 1, 3, 5, 7).

SUMMARY AND CONCLUSIONS.

The botanical composition of the herbage of pastures on two types of soil has been studied in considerable detail with respect to the history of individual species by the Percentage Frequency and the Specific Frequency methods.   Five areas

[1] On Area 8, on the sites of burnt gorse bushes.

have been investigated, three of them several times in consecutive years, on one type, and three areas on the other type. The history of each area has been given, and also in the case of six of the areas the chief details of the seeds-mixtures used in laying them down to grass (Table IV., p. 16a).

Some variation has been found in the behaviour of the same species on different areas on the same soil type, and considerable differences on the different soil types.

In drawing conclusions for the two area groups it is necessary to bear in mind not only that they are not comparable in soil, but that their history is also quite different. Areas 1-4 have been in regular cultivation on the long rotation system, so that relatively short-lived plants would tend to be perpetuated, while more permanent plants, unless capable of surviving cultivation, would be eradicated or would have no chance of recolonising the ground unless especially adapted. These areas are also in constant communication with other parts of the farm, and particularly with the farm buildings, as they are largely grazed by cattle, so that although perhaps not actually manured they are still affected by their position. Even Area 5, which had been under grass for a long period prior to the rotation during which it was examined, would have been affected by its proximity to the farm buildings, and all these areas are practically surrounded by land treated in the same way.

Areas 6 and 7, on the other hand, had only been through one period of cultivation since they had been for a long period in the grass-heath condition. They were also remote from the farm buildings, and formed part of a sheep-walk. There was practically no communication between them and the land under regular cultivation, and they were almost entirely[1] surrounded by grass-heath or by uncultivated land. In this case, therefore, plants which are short-lived under the grass-heath conditions would have disappeared, and even when the land was brought under cultivation they would not easily be re-introduced. This is probably why

---

[1] Entirely except for a few yards where Area 7 joins the cultivable part of the field in which Area 4 is situated.

such plants as *Ranunculus repens, Bellis perennis* and *Cynosurus cristatus* were so poorly represented on Area 7, and in the case of the two former plants, on Area 6.

THE EFFECT OF ALTITUDE, SLOPE, ASPECT, ETC.

Since, as shown above, the two groups of areas differed very greatly in what appear to be more important respects, the influence of these factors can not accurately be estimated. The most marked differences that may be traceable to these are, that *Festuca rubra* is very prevalent on Areas 1-4, but negligible on Areas 6-8, and that both *Agrostis alba* and *A. tenuis* occurred on the former areas and only *A. tenuis* on the latter.

THE EFFECT OF CULTIVATION.

Areas 6 and 7 were similarly treated throughout their period of cultivation, so that the effect of this can not be seen in their case. At the same time, it is very difficult to believe that the great difference between the herbage of the two areas was entirely due to the difference in the composition of the seeds-mixtures, but there is no evidence to the contrary.

From the results for these areas, one point in particular becomes prominent, viz., that the inclusion of a cleaning crop is not necessarily the only means of eradicating undesirable plants. As will be seen from a comparison of the results for Areas 6 and 8, the disappearance of the grass-heath plants from Area 6 was remarkable. In particular, the suppression of *Agrostis tenuis* may be noted, as this grass is generally considered to be perhaps the most difficult of all to get rid of. Thus, although the writer has several times used the words "imperfectly cleaned" to indicate land which had not been under a cleaning crop, the distinction does not seem to be absolute.

Areas 1, 2 and 3 were not cultivated in exactly the same way. Even Area 2, however, although it had not been under a cleaning crop, had been carefully cleaned as far as growing cereal crops in succession allowed. On these areas, some results, such as the greater prominence of *Festuca rubra*, and the occurrence of particular plants on Area 2 in greater abundance than on other areas, and the smaller proportion of *Agrostis* spp. in the early history of Areas 1 and 3, and also possibly the greater prevalence of some miscellaneous plants such as *Ranunculus repens*, *Bellis perennis*, etc., on Area 3, have been considered as showing the effect of different forms of cultivation.

THE EFFECT OF AFTER-TREATMENT.

It has been suggested that this might have been to some extent the cause of the difference between Areas 6 and 7, but on consideration, the suggestion has not been found tenable. A difference in manuring has left some distinct results, but on these areas it did not affect any species very materially except *Trifolium repens*, and even in the case of this plant the effect was only temporary.

THE EFFECT OF SEEDS-MIXTURES.

On Areas 1-4 few marked differences traceable to this cause were met with. A difference in the quantity of the seed of some species, such as *Dactylis glomerata*, seems to have had some lasting effect, but in the case of other plants, such as *Lolium perenne*, the effect was generally at most temporary. The inclusion of the seeds of some plants which are for some reason exotic to the areas on which they were sown had some marked results. Thus, although it did not change the character of the herbage to any appreciable extent, *Festuca elatior* persisted for at least $9\frac{1}{2}$ years on Area 2. The most marked results were obtained, however, by the inclusion of the seeds of *Cynosurus cristatus* and *Anthoxanthum odoratum* in the seeds-mixture for Area 6.

On the other hand, the seeds of some exotic plants, such as *Festuca duriuscula* and *Arrhenatherum elatius*, were practically useless.

It is quite obvious from these results that the seeds-mixtures used on Areas 1-4 and on Area 7 at least were not successful after five or six years. It is true that some desirable plants made

their appearance in some quantity at this time, but a large proportion of undesirable plants also appeared, and taking Area 2
as an example, it would seem that the seeds *Cynosurus crsistatus*
and *Poa trivialis* at least should also have been included in the
seeds-mixture, so that they might not start at a disadvantage in
competition with other plants. It is probable also that the
inclusion of a greater quantity *Festuca elatior* and (or) its variety
F. elatior var. *pratensis* would give good results. On the other
hand, *Festuca duriuscula* might have been excluded, and also
possibly *Poa pratensis*, *Trifolium repens* and *Anthyllis Vulneraria*.
In this case, it would seem to be quite unnecessary to add
Achillea Millefolium, but it might apparently have been included
with advantage in the seeds-mixtures for Areas 6 and 7, while
Carum Petroselinum and *Arrhenatherum elatius* might have been
omitted.

REFERENCES.

(1) ARMSTRONG, S. F.: The Botanical and Chemical Composi- of the Herbage of Pasture and Meadows. *Jour. Agr. Sci.*, vol. ii., 1907.

(2) ARMSTRONG, S. F.: *British Grasses and their Employment in Agriculture.* Camb. Univ. Press, 1917.

(3) BRENCHLEY, W. E.: Buried Weed Seeds. *Journ. Agr. Sci.*, vol. ix., 1918.

(4) CROWTHER, C., and RUSTON, A. G.: The Influence on Crop and Soil of Manures applied to Permanent Meadow. *Ib.* vol. vii., 1915-16.

(5) *Cyclopedia of Modern Agriculture, The Standard*: Gresham Publ. Co., London, 1911.

(6) HALL, A. D., and RUSSELL, E. J.: On the Causes of High Nutritive Value and Fertility of the Fatting Pastures of Romney Marsh. *Journ. Agr. Sci.*, vol. iv., 1911-12.

(7) HUNTER, JAMES: *35th Price List of Agricultural Seeds.* Chester, 1917.

(8) JENKIN, T. J.: *Seed-Testing and Report on Seeds Tested in* 1913-15. Univ. Coll. of N. Wales, Bangor, 1916.

(9) JENKIN, T. J.: Ordinary White Clover Seed *v.* Wild White Clover Seed. *Journ. Bd. Agr.*, vol. xxiii., March, 1917.

(10) JONES, A. E., and STAPLEDON, R. G.: *The Improvement of Upland Pastures.* Univ. Coll., Aberystwyth, 1916.

(11) Official Seed-Testing Station: First Annual Report. *Journ. Bd. Agr.*, vol. xxv., Sept., 1918.

(12) *Report on Nationalities and Varieties of Red Clover.* Univ. of Leeds and Yorkshire Council for Agr. Educ., Bulletin 57, 1906.

(13) SOMERVILLE, WILLIAM: Influence on the Production of Mutton of Manures applied to Pastures. *Journ. Bd. Agr. Supplement,* vol. xvii., Jan., 1911.

(14) STAPLEDON, R. G. : *Report on the Condition of the Seed Trade in the Aberystwyth College Area.* Univ. Coll., Aberystwyth, 1914.

(15) STAPLEDON, R. G. : Pasture Problems : Drought Resistance. *Journ. Agr. Sci.,* vol. v., 1913.

(16) STAPLEDON, R. G. : Pasture Problems : The Response of Individual Species under Manures. *Ib.,* vol. vi., 1914.

(17) STAPLEDON, R. G. : On the Plant Communities of Farm Land. *Annals Bot.,* vol. xxx., 1916.

(18) STAPLEDON, R. G., and JENKIN, T. J. : Pasture Problems : Indigenous Species in Relation to Habitat and Sown Species. *Journ. Agr. Sci.,* vol. viii., 1916.

(19) SUTTON, MARTIN J. : *Permanent and Temporary Pastures.* London : Simpkin, Marshall. Popular Edition, 1902.

(20) *Sutton's Farmers' Year Book.* Reading: Sutton & Sons, 1919.

(21) TANSLEY, A. G. : *Types of British Vegetation.* Camb. Univ. Press, 1911.

(22) YAPP, R. H., JOHNS, D., and JONES, O. T. : The Salt Marshes of the Dovey Estuary. *Journ. Ecology,* vol. iv., 1916, and vol. v., 1917.

(23) JENKIN, T. J. : Unpublished Results.

ImTheStory.com

Personalized Classic Books in many genre's

Unique gift for kids, partners, friends, colleagues

Customize:

- Character Names
- Upload your own front/back cover images (optional)
- Inscribe a personal message/dedication on the inside page (optional)

Customize many titles Including
- Alice in Wonderland
- Romeo and Juliet
- The Wizard of Oz
- A Christmas Carol
- Dracula
- Dr. Jekyll & Mr. Hyde
- And more...

Lightning Source UK Ltd.
Milton Keynes UK
UKOW07f0914020115

243865UK00019B/588/P